Doug Wagner

Boas

Everything about Selection, Care, Nutrition,
Diseases, Breeding, and Behavior

With 53 Color Photographs

Illustrations by David Wenzel

BARRON'S

About the Author

Doug Wagner is a computer programmer who has kept and bred snakes for over 20 years. He is currently the president of the Suncoast Herpetological Society, based in Clearwater, Florida, and organizes the annual Florida International Reptile Show, in Tampa. He maintains a medium-sized collection of 50 to 60 snakes, primarily boas and pythons.

© Copyright 1996 by Barron's Educational Series, Inc.

All inquiries should be addressed to:
Barron's Educational Series, Inc.
250 Wireless Boulevard
Hauppauge, NY 11788

International Standard Book No. 0-8120-9626-6

Library of Congress Catalog Card No. 96-1187

Library of Congress Cataloging-in-Publication Data

Wagner, Doug.
    Boas : everything about acquisition, care, nutrition, diseases, breeding, and behavior / Doug Wagner.
        p.   cm.—(A complete pet owner's manual)
    Includes bibliographical references (p.) and index.
    ISBN 0-8120-9626-6
    1. Boa constrictors as pets. 2. Boidae.
3. Snakes as pets. I. Title. II. Series.
SF459.S5W34   1996
639.3'96—dc20   96-1187
                              CIP

Printed in Hong Kong

9876

Photo Credits

R.D. Bartlett: pages 8 top, 21 top, 64 top, 65, 66, 69 top left and right, bottom left, 73 top and bottom, 74 top, 75, 76, 78 top, 81 bottom, 82 bottom, 85; Zig Leszczynski: front cover, inside front cover, back cover (upper left, upper right, bottom right), pages 4, 12, 17, 29, 44, 53, 64 bottom, 67 top, 74 bottom, 79, 82 top, 83, 86 bottom; Bill Love, Glades Herp, Inc.: back cover (bottom left), pages 8 bottom, 9, 25, 28, 48, 68, 72 top and bottom, 80, 84, 86 top; Carl Switak: pages 21 bottom, 32, 36 top and bottom, 49, 67 bottom, 69 bottom right, 70, 71, 77, 78 bottom, 81 top.

Photos on the Covers

Front cover: emerald tree boa; inside front cover: boa constrictor; inside back cover: Peruvian redtail boa; back cover: Brazilian rainbow boa (upper left), albino boa constrictor (upper right), newborn Dumeril's boa (bottom left), Kenyan sand boa (bottom right).

Important Note

The subject of this book is the keeping and care of nonpoisonous snakes. Snake keepers should realize, however, that even the bite of a snake regarded as nonpoisonous can have harmful consequences. So see a doctor immediately after any snake bite.

Handling giant serpents requires a lot of experience and a great sense of responsibility. Carelessness can be deadly! Inexperienced snake keepers and snake keepers who have small children are therefore urgently advised not to keep giant serpents.

Electrical appliances used in the care of snakes must carry a valid "UL approved" marking. Everyone using such equipment should be aware of the dangers involved with it. It is strongly recommended that you purchase a device that will instantly shut off the electrical current in the event of failure in the appliances or wiring. A circuit-protection device with a similar function has to be installed by a licensed electrician.

Contents

Preface

Can a snake affect your life? I should say it can, especially if your first experience is a good one. Over 20 years ago I caught my very first snake, a small banded water snake. Basically, it was all an accident and a misunderstanding. I was in a rowboat catching turtles with a dip net, not looking for snakes. Someone had told me there were no venomous snakes in the area. I watched, entranced, as the snake crawled over the lily pads next to the boat. What was an 11-year-old to do? I picked it up, it didn't bite, and the rest, as they say, is history.

For me, the progression from native colubrids (rat snakes, kingsnakes, etc.) to more exotic boas took only two years. At that time, a boa meant a common boa constrictor. Most of the more than 50 species and subspecies mentioned in this book were unheard of in those days—but even a common boa was everything but common to a boy of 13. It was beautiful, and it was exotic. Herpetologists, scientists who study reptiles and amphibians (or "herps"), never did care for amateurs and non-scientists using their title, and the term *herpetoculturist*, a person who keeps or breeds reptiles, would not be coined for many years. Snake keeper, reptile hobbyist, or whatever I was, I felt like a serious one.

My collection has fluctuated greatly in size and species over the years, but has rarely been without at least one form of boa. Their slow pace, docile nature, infrequent defecation, excellent feeding characteristics, and tendency to remain in the open make them superb pets and display animals, offset only by the large size of some species. I have felt fortunate to be a part of the recent explosion in herpetoculture that has not only resulted in tremendous advances in the quality of reptile care, but has also made available many never-before-seen animals from around the world, including new and exciting varieties of boas. Small to moderate-sized species now abound for the boa fancier with the vision to concede that he or she is not prepared to maintain an 8- to 10-foot (2–3 m) adult boa constrictor.

Regardless of the type of boa chosen, the information, enclosures, and accessories required to successfully keep them are now easily acquired. If you are considering the purchase of your first boa, or if you already own one or more, it is the goal of this book to help you understand your options and make informed decisions, and to ensure that your snakes live long and healthy lives. It is also the goal of this book to discourage those who see a pet boa constrictor as a disposable novelty. If we are to put such beautiful animals into cages for our enjoyment, then surely we owe them much in return.

Considerations Before Buying

Why a Boa?

For the experienced herpetoculturist ready to advance into the world of exotics, perhaps no snake represents a finer choice than a boa. Truly beautiful animals, their gentle demeanor and relative ease of maintenance have for decades made them popular pets the world over. But even though many varieties can be housed with a minimum of specialized care, it must always be remembered that boas are still exotics, adapted to survive in their particular environment, not ours. Keeping them healthy in captivity requires a commitment to meet their needs. This is not to say that you will need to recreate a portion of the Amazon rainforest in your home. Such an elaborate setup would only present maintenance headaches to you and cleanliness problems for your boa. You will, however, have to consider factors such as temperature, humidity, and photoperiod. In addition to your obligations to your boa come obligations to yourself and to those around you to be a responsible snake owner. If you fully understand these obligations and are prepared to meet the challenge, then a boa could be for you.

If you are considering the purchase of your very first snake, a boa may or may not be the best choice. For that matter, a snake may not even be your best choice for a pet. For example, are you prepared to feed it cute little animals such as mice, rats, or rabbits? There is no alternative. Can you accept getting bitten occasionally? I have enjoyed keeping snakes for over 20 years, but I recognize that it is not for everyone. Your first snake could get you hooked for life, or put you off snake-keeping forever. If you are a beginner, I urge you to learn as much as you can before you buy, and to carefully evaluate your reasons for choosing a boa and your ability to keep it healthy. The following sections are intended to help you make an informed decision. If after reading them you are still not sure, then consider easing into your new hobby with an equally docile, yet smaller and cheaper snake, such as a rat snake or kingsnake.

The poorest reason of all for obtaining a boa is to impress others. If you eagerly anticipate the attention and reaction to your new pet, I strongly urge you to reconsider. While small snakes may be tolerable even to people who fear them, large snakes often make them uneasy. The appearance of any large constrictor in public, whether escaped, set free, or in the hands of an irresponsible owner, puts the entire herpetocultural community at risk. The media thrive on sensationalism, and big snakes make big news. Every incident involving irresponsible snake ownership has high potential for making the front page, and gives further ammunition to those who would have our hobby banned completely. If attention is what you crave, buy a flashy red sports car instead.

Size

Boas, along with pythons and anacondas, comprise a group often referred to as the *giant* snakes. Of these three, boas attain the shortest maximum length, and like pythons, not all boa species qualify as giants. Some, such as the rosy boas and sand boas, grow to just 2 to 3 feet (.6–.9 m), while only a few boa constrictor subspecies from South America are capable of exceeding 10 feet (3 m). The commonly accepted record for a boa constrictor is an 18½-foot-long (5.6 m) red-tail boa. Rarely will one exceed 12 feet (3.7 m) in captivity, with 8 to 10 feet (2–3 m) being more common. Somewhere in between the small and the large are a number of mid-size boas, including Dumeril's boas, rainbow boas, and for more advanced herpetoculturists, tree boas (see species accounts, beginning on page 63).

Before purchasing one of the medium to large boa species, consider the full impact of its adult size. With proper feeding, that handsome little boa constrictor in the 10-gallon (38 L) aquarium will require a 20-gallon (76 L) aquarium by the end of its first year, and will rapidly progress through increasingly larger enclosures until a 5- or 6-foot (1.5–1.8 m) cage is needed. Floor space is not the only issue. Large cages can be expensive, as well as heavy and cumbersome to move and clean. A big snake consumes big meals, and, if I may point out, defecates big messes! Depending on its thickness and absorbency, the entire cage substrate may be soaked and require replacement. Where will you put the snake while you clean its cage? A large boa is a powerful constrictor, capable of wrapping itself around furniture, fixtures, or people. Putting one back into its cage can often turn into a wrestling match, typically with the animal becoming more

Some boa constrictors can grow to over 10 feet (3 m). The proper way to hold a large boa is to support the body in several places. Avoid placing such large snakes around your neck.

and more agitated. A very large specimen is capable of causing death should it wrap around a person's neck and constrict, although deaths from boas are almost unheard of, and likely the result of extreme carelessness on the part of the handler and the snake's fear of falling rather than any actual intent to do harm. Proper caution will reduce your risk to near zero.

As with any pet, boas may occasionally bite the hand that feeds them. Despite their gentle nature, even the most docile boa can be startled or mistake your hand for a tasty rodent. Multiple rows of sharp teeth are capable of inflicting a painful bite, especially from a large specimen. A typical defensive bite is quick, and over before you can react, but in a feeding response the snake may not release immediately. The natural reaction to pull away a hand may do additional damage to you or cause injury to the snake.

Defensive posture of gaping mouth and hissing, sometimes bluff and sometimes not, is common to many boa constrictors, like this Argentine boa.

One last consideration regarding size: What are your future plans? Your boa may live 20 years or longer. Marriage, college, job transfers, and having children are just a few of the

Captive-bred boas, like this juvenile Guyana red-tail boa constrictor, are usually healthier than imported specimens.

lifestyle changes that could impact your collection. If the time arrives when your snake must go, you may find the market for a sizable boa constrictor to be quite small, and your local zoo or animal pound will probably not be interested. But don't even consider releasing your boa in the woods; not only is it irresponsible and cruel—in most places it's illegal.

Temperament

The overwhelming popularity of boas attests to their gentle disposition. Few species of snakes calm down as quickly and completely after birth. With a reasonable amount of human inter-action, most boas will retain their good-natured demeanor throughout life. Exceptions do exist, however, at the individual and the species level. The best way to avoid the occasional boa with a bad attitude is to select a healthy juvenile, and simply spend a little extra time before buying, holding the animal in a relaxed manner and observing its behavior.

Imported, wild-caught adults are often irritable and take time to adjust to cap-tivity. Such imports may also be finicky eaters, and commonly harbor internal and external parasites. They are there-fore best left to experienced keepers knowledgeable about the detection and treatment of these conditions.

Not all boa species contribute to the docile reputation of the group. The Amazon tree boas, emerald tree boas, and even a few boa constrictor sub-species have somewhat questionable reputations. These should also be left to experienced keepers. Notes on tem-perament have been provided for each boa profiled in the section beginning on page 63.

Wild-Caught Versus Captive-Bred

As already mentioned, wild-caught boas, especially adults, often harbor a number of internal and external parasites, requiring a quarantine period, medical examination, and appropriate treatment. Imported adults may not acclimate well to captivity, remaining irritable and refusing to eat. Unless you are an advanced breeder in need of a new genetic bloodline, I would always recommend purchasing a captive-bred boa whenever possible.

The advantages of captive-bred boas begin with the health of the parents, which are often long-term captives themselves. The care of the neonates from the moment of birth, and a shorter time period from source to final destination, increases the likelihood that captive-bred boas are healthy.

Sometimes the distinction between captive-bred, captive-born, and wild-caught becomes confused. This is the case with many of the juvenile boa constrictors seen in pet shops today. Gravid females collected in South America are placed in holding facilities until they give birth, making the offspring technically captive-born. Imported gravid females may also give birth after arriving in-country. The low prices resulting from so many juvenile boas being imported mean that it is not always financially feasible for breeders to commit their time and resources to producing them. A pet shop buying its stock from an animal wholesaler may not know the source of the boas it offers. Imported juveniles, whether wild-caught or captive-born, are much less likely to present as many problems as imported adults, but are still subject to stress, diseases, and parasites during holding and shipping.

Where to Buy Your Boa

Finding boa constrictors has always been as easy as visiting your neighborhood pet shop. The vast majority of those seen are common boa constrictors (*Boa constrictor imperator*), some-times referred to as Colombian or Central American boas, which are imported in large numbers for the pet trade. Few pet shops carry other types of boas, although red-tail boa constrictors (*Boa constrictor constrictor*), rainbow boas (*Epicrates cenchria*), and rosy boas (*Lichanura trivirgata*) are occasionally seen.

In recent years, the captive breeding of snakes has exploded into a major industry, making every type of boa more obtainable. Just browse through any reptile magazine's ads or classifieds to find a veritable *Who's Who* of the industry's top breeders, many of whom will gladly provide a free price list upon request. Access to breeders in your own area can be as easy as visiting or joining the closest herpetological society. Chances are good that you'll find some breeders among the members, or at the very least get some recommendations.

As the number of breeders continues to grow, regional reptile breeders' shows have become major annual events, springing up in a number of states and in other countries as well. Usually held in late summer and fall, to coincide with the hatching and birth of most snakes, these shows allow the

Reptile shows are an excellent source of boas and everything needed to keep them healthy. This is the Florida International Reptile Show, organized by the author each September in Tampa.

public to buy breeder-direct and to meet and learn from the breeders themselves. Most reptile magazines regularly publish a calendar of such events.

Also seen more and more frequently are specialty pet stores dealing exclusively with reptiles and reptile-related merchandise. Reptile stores typically offer a variety of imported and captive-bred animals. A reputable store will not hesitate to tell you the source of the boa you are interested in buying.

Mail-Order Snakes?

If ordering snakes by mail sounds a bit risky, that's because it is. But it can also provide you with access to some of the best and most respected breeders in the country, no matter where they are. Snakes are not actually mailed to your door, but shipped as air freight to your nearest major airport for pick up. Because you will not be able to inspect the animals yourself for appearance and health, it is most important that you deal only with a reputable supplier. References from your friends or members of a herpetological society are a good place to start. A reputable supplier will guarantee that animals will arrive alive and in good health, and may also guarantee that the animal will have no defects for an additional 10 to 30 days. While good health may be an absolute, what constitutes a "beautiful" snake is purely subjective. If appearance is critical to you, look for a breeder who will supply pictures of available snakes; be prepared to pay a small charge for the pictures. Once you have established a good relationship with a supplier as a regular paying customer, you can inquire about obtaining their best picks from new litters.

Shipping

If you are unfamiliar with the process of shipping snakes, provide your supplier with the name of your nearest major airport and he or she will be happy to explain the procedure. You will need to choose a method of payment, usually credit card, check, or C.O.D. Using a credit card avoids C.O.D. charges and the delay of mailing a personal check and waiting for it to clear. Shipping charges may be added, although some suppliers will pay for shipping on orders over a certain amount. Your supplier will tell you what time the animals will be delivered to his or her airport, the airline(s) to be used, an airbill number, and estimated arrival time at your chosen airport. Using a single airline and a direct flight between only two airports is always the cheapest and safest method. Because freight is often shipped on a space-available basis, an exact arrival time is rarely possible to obtain. Premium shipping with a guaranteed arrival time is usually available at a higher cost, and should be considered during extremely hot or cold weather. If your supplier ships out early in the morning, same-day receipt may be possible; otherwise, expect your shipment to arrive on the following day. At the estimated arrival time, call the freight office of the airline and inquire about the status of your shipment using your airbill number. When your shipment arrives, pick it up as soon as possible, especially in bad weather, as freight terminals are huge warehouses with loading doors open to the elements, sometimes 24 hours a day.

Snakes are typically transported in individual cloth bags, or in shallow plastic cups with crumpled paper towels or newspaper as a cushion. These containers are then placed into an insulating styrofoam shipping box with more crumpled newspaper as a cushion, and small holes to allow air exchange. A chemical heat pack may be included during cold weather. Open your shipment and inspect it at the cargo office. If anything is amiss, fill out a discrepancy report with the airline personnel and call your supplier for further instructions. Failure to do so may void any guarantee.

Ordering snakes by phone may be a bit risky, and every shipment arrives accompanied by at least some trepidation. But by doing your homework beforehand, and being very clear with your chosen supplier as to what you are looking for, the experience can be very rewarding.

Cost

As with all things, the cost of any snake species is affected by supply and demand. Factors determining supply include the number of animals held in collections, ease of breeding, average litter size, and quantities imported, whereas demand often relates to attractiveness, temperament, rarity, and price. Juveniles will cost less than yearlings or older specimens. Buying a yearling can be advantageous when selecting future breeding stock, because it helps to avoid any unwanted color shifts that can occur as a snake grows. However, you will pay extra for the previous owner's risk and care in raising the animal for a year, and a yearling is more likely than a juvenile to have been exposed to parasites or diseases.

Snakes that are easily bred and produce large litters tend to flood the market and quickly drive down prices. Although well-documented in colubrids and some types of pythons, this has rarely been a problem with boas; however, the high demand for boa constrictors has been met in recent years by the equally high numbers being imported, keeping prices relatively low. For other boa species in high demand, where few or no specimens are imported and captive breeding is not yet widespread, costs remain high. A good example of this are the boas from the island of Madagascar. When countries restrict or eliminate the export of animals, prices climb until breeders are able to satisfy the demand.

Through selective breeding and the occasional surprise import or offspring, new and unusual color and pattern morphs regularly appear on breeders' price lists, typically accompanied by hefty price tags. In the early 1990s, juvenile albino boa constrictors appeared on the market at a whopping price of $10,000 each! Fortunately for those to whom normal coloration and pattern have an appeal all their own, a common boa constrictor can often be acquired for less than $100, while the attractive true red-tails can cost a few hundred dollars.

With a bit of research at pet shops, reptile stores, breeders' shows, and your local herpetological society, and by checking the classified ads and requesting price lists advertised in reptile magazines, you should have no trouble finding a boa to match your budget.

Regulations

Several levels of regulation may affect your ability to own a snake, or a particular species of snake. The first hits close to home. If you rent a house or apartment, check your lease to be sure that keeping snakes is not prohibited. Next, check the local ordinances of your city or town. This can often be accomplished by a visit to your local library or city hall, or a call to your police department. If the law prohibits keeping snakes or exotics, don't give up. How old is the law? How many others do you know who keep or wish to keep snakes? Enlist the help of your local herp society and consult with city officials about getting the law changed. Be courteous, be ready with facts, and be ready to compromise if necessary.

State wildlife agencies, besides protecting threatened or endangered

Most boa constrictors found in pet shops are common boas (Boa constrictor imperator), usually from Colombia.

native species, often set rules pertaining to animal housing and transportation. These rules may affect cage size and design, limit snake length, or restrict the number of animals kept or housed together. A permit to keep snakes may be required. Check the government section of your phone book for the number of the appropriate state wildlife agency.

National and international regulations, such as the Endangered Species Act and the Convention on International Trade in Endangered

For snakes that are unfamiliar or known to bite, use a firm but gentle grasp behind the head. Such restraint is also required for force-feeding, inspecting the mouth, or removing unshed eyecaps.

Species (CITES), restrict, prohibit, or require additional paperwork for the importation, transport, or keeping of endangered species. With their business at stake, however, it is unlikely that your pet shop or reptile store is offering illegal specimens.

Finally, if you are lucky enough to live in a community that allows responsible snake ownership, don't be the cause of your own undoing. Many pet restrictions are the result of unfortunate incidents that stir public anti-snake sentiment. Keep the hobby reputable and legal for those herpetoculturists who will follow us.

Choosing a Healthy Snake

If you have thought it through and concluded that a boa is right for you, and that you are right for a boa, then let's make sure you get a healthy one. If you are a novice, consider having a more knowledgeable person help you make your choice. Before you even touch it, examine your candidate and its enclosure. Is the cage filthy? Do any of its cagemates look sick? Look for partially open mouths, wheezing, and bubbles or discharge from the nostrils. These are symptoms that should send you to another cage, or to another source altogether. Respiratory diseases are often contagious, with the potential to wipe out an entire collection. Never buy a sick boa with the hope of doctoring it back to health.

Look closely around the eyes and along the back. Tiny moving brown or black dots are mites, bloodsucking parasites that spread quickly and can infest an entire reptile collection (see Mites, page 56). Fine, white specks may be mite droppings. A heavy white powder may mean that mites are being treated with Sevin Dust, a common garden pesticide. If you are willing, and your candidate is otherwise healthy, mites can be effectively treated during the quarantine period.

Now it is time to pick up your future pet. Check again for the above symptoms. Also check the mental groove, a narrow gap between the scales under the chin, as it is a favorite spot for mites. Your boa should be crawling slowly in your hands, its tongue flicking steadily. The body should be smooth and firm, free of sores, scars, or unusual lumps. The eyes should be bright, clear, and alert, and the mouth should close completely and naturally. Grasping the snake firmly but gently behind the head, carefully force the mouth open with the side of a pen or other smooth, thin object. The mouth should be clean and light pink or white, free of open lesions, discoloration, or cheesy material that could indicate mouth rot.

Finally, ask the seller for any additional information regarding your boa, such as when and what your snake ate last, and if it has shed recently. Is it a male or female? Most reptile stores and breeders sell their offspring correctly sexed, or will make the determination on the spot. If you are unsure about anything, now is the time to ask.

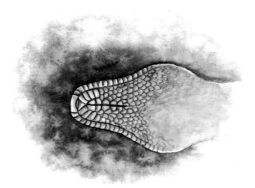

The mental groove under the chin is a favorite spot for mites.

Your Responsibilities Begin

Now that you have joined the proud ranks of boa owners, it is time to get your snake home and set up. A cloth bag such as a pillowcase, tied at the top, is ideal for transporting your new pet. Do not place the bag on the dashboard, or run into the grocery store and leave it in a hot car. Excessive heat can cause death within minutes.

Have a cage waiting when you arrive home, in a separate room from any other reptiles already owned. A one- to three-month quarantine period should be used to evaluate a new arrival and ensure that it is disease-free. If new arrivals are added during the quarantine period, the process starts anew for all snakes in the same room. Even if you plan to house your boa in a large or elaborate cage, you should use a small temporary cage during the quarantine period, with only a hide box, a water dish big enough to soak in, and newspaper for substrate. If mites are found, you'll be glad you kept your new snake in simple quarters.

Your new boa has been stressed, so resist the urge to hold it or look in on it too often. Give it a few days to get acclimated to its new environment. A temperature of 83 to 86°F (28–30°C) is optimum at this time, aiding any unfinished digestion and boosting the immune system. Do not try to feed it for the first week. If you have other reptiles, always clean and handle quarantined animals last. Wash your hands when finished, and never transfer cage items or uneaten food from your quarantine area to your main collection. Watch for mites, either on the snake or drowned in the water dish, and, if found, begin treatment as suggested under the section of this book on external parasites (beginning on page 56).

Keeping Records

Whether you maintain a single snake or a large collection, keeping records can add to your overall enjoyment and knowledge. For large collections, it is almost essential. In its simplest form, record keeping should include the dates and details of events such as feeding, defecation, shedding, medical observations, and treatments. To get even more benefits, record water changes, temperature readings (especially when associated with unusual behavior), and periodic length and weight measurements as well. As patterns become apparent, "norms" are established. Exceptions to these norms raise questions that might otherwise not be asked. Why has my snake not defecated for two weeks when it normally does so within a few days after eating? Why does my snake stop eating in November—it did the same thing last year? The records themselves often provide the answer to the questions. For example, your boa regurgitates after eating three rats. Is it sick? According to your records, the snake normally eats two rats, and also regurgitated the last time you gave it three. There's your answer. When any snake of mine refuses to eat, the first thing I check is its shedding pattern; often the snake feels and reacts to the onset of a shedding cycle before the telltale cloudiness appears. Records can help you remember and repeat successful husbandry practices when new specimens are acquired much later. They can also supply critical information to your veterinarian when problems arise.

The easiest and most widely used system of record keeping is the use of individual index cards for each specimen. Each card is kept on or beside the animal's enclosure so that record keeping is easy and automatic, and the card easily transferred when the snake is moved to a new enclosure. As cards are filled up, they are replaced with new ones, and eventually filed away. Every keeper has his or her own method of notation, using letters, abbreviations, or symbols to speed up the process and save space—a "W" for a water change, or perhaps "2M-10g" for eating two mice weighing 10 grams each. Records should also include date, or at least year, of birth, the source from which the snake was obtained, and, especially if breeding is anticipated, any known lineage. Many breeders assign each snake a code number, which when tracked properly can be used to prevent the purchase and inbreeding of related animals. When purchasing from a breeder, request the code numbers for the parents and record them.

Careful records not only establish norms for individual specimens, but for entire species and subspecies as well. From the records of dedicated herpetoculturists, both amateur and professional, have come some of the most important discoveries and techniques for successful husbandry.

The Perils of a Large Collection

Before we go any further, and if you intend to have a large collection, please be aware of the following possible drawbacks.

Snakes, in their infinite variety, are like the proverbial Lays potato chip—it's hard to be satisfied with just one. If your first experience with a pet snake is a good one, and I sincerely hope it is, the chances are good that you'll get the urge to try your hand at breeding it, or to explore additional species as well. What we all have to remember is that these are not coins or stamps that can be collected with little more effort than an initial outlay of cash, but living, breathing animals that are fully dependent on us for their very lives. Unless you are willing and able to devote the same amount of time, attention, and care to each new arrival, your snakes will begin suffering from neglect. Cages may get cleaned less often or not as thoroughly. Handling becomes less frequent, often involving no more than the snake being picked up or shoved aside during cleaning, resulting in a previously docile snake reverting to its instinctive, defensive ways. As collections increase, cage sizes decrease. The dangers of parasites and diseases are compounded and their treatment made more difficult. Less frequent close observation can mean that symptoms of distress or disease go unnoticed.

Perhaps every serious herpetoculturist is destined to commence his or her own search for the perfect reptile, but that species just might not exist. It may be a tough decision, but when daily care becomes an assembly-line chore rather than a relaxing pastime, it is time to reevaluate your priorities. Decide which species within your collection are the closest to your ideal, and consider selling off the rest. Even if you can handle a large collection, keeping snakes with similar caging, feeding, and breeding requirements can simplify your hobby and make things more pleasant for both you and your pets. Many successful breeders have opted for depth instead of breadth, specializing in a single or specific group of related species—boas, pythons, tricolor kingsnakes, etc.

Breeding snakes may appear to be a fun path to easy riches, but it involves a lot of time, hard work, risk, aggravation, and frustration. A week of vacation is not a big issue with a pet snake or two, yet it may be out of the question when a large collection is involved. It takes several years of careful selection and culling of undesirable animals to establish a worthy breeding group. Snakes that won't breed, and neonates that won't eat, can push your patience to the limit. Even if your breeding efforts are successful, finding outlets for the offspring can be difficult. The competition is fierce, sometimes driving prices down so low as to make breeding a particular species financially unrewarding. Until you become established and earn a reputation as a breeder of high quality and character, you may have to settle for selling many of your offspring at wholesale prices to pet shops, reptile stores, or jobbers (pet shop suppliers). If your goal is to breed snakes as your career, be prepared to build or rent a separate facility, hire help, and incorporate your business. Many have tried, only to sell off everything within two years.

Understanding Boas

Basic Anatomy

If you are new to herpetoculture, understanding the basic anatomy and needs of snakes will help explain how and why they do some of the things they do, and what you will need to provide in order to successfully keep them in captivity.

Snakes are reptiles. Like all reptiles, they are ectothermic (cold-blooded) and have dry, scaly skin. The scales are actually tough folds of skin, not plates that can be scraped off, as on a fish. Most boas have smooth scales, although some have keeled scales, with a central ridge that produces an overall rough texture. Some boas have a combination of both types. Not having to generate heat internally greatly reduces the body's demand for fuel, but requires that snakes spend much of their time

A primitive family of snakes, boas still retain vestigial pelvic bones, often terminating in spurs visible on either side of the anal vent. Typically longer on males, the spurs are often used in mating.

utilizing external heat sources for regulating body temperature to the optimum level for muscle activity, digestion, and disease resistance. While the sun provides the necessary heat directly from above, solar collectors such as rocks, logs, roads, and even the ground itself can accelerate the process from below, allowing the snake to reduce its exposure in the open and to spend more time on daily activities of searching for food, water, or a mate. When things get too hot, snakes will search out shade or water, or go underground where it is cooler. This need for self-thermoregulation is carried over into captivity. Whether heat is provided from above or below, it is a crucial component of successful husbandry.

Over their long course of evolution, snakes have lost more than just legs. Ears and even the entire left lung have virtually disappeared in many species. Other paired organs, like kidneys and

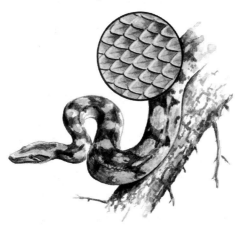

Keeled scales have a ridge down the center.

ovaries or testis, have been moved around to get in line, instead of residing side by side. The taxonomic family Boidae, which includes the subfamilies *Boinae* (true boas), *Erycinae* (sand, rosy, and rubber boas), and *Pythoninae* (pythons), is a group of primitive, less-evolved snakes. Boids still retain a functional left lung and vestiges of the pelvic girdle. Small claws, or spurs, remnants of the hind legs, can often be found on either side of the snake's cloaca, particularly on males. The family Tropidophidae (dwarf boas), though no longer grouped with the Boidae, exhibits many boa traits, but also more highly evolved characteristics, such as the absence of the left lung.

An incredibly flexible jaw, elastic skin, and long stomach allow snakes to take advantage of huge sizes and quantities of prey when available, while an efficient digestive system and slow metabolism ensure survival during long, lean periods. A sensitive tongue that tastes the air, and in some species sensory pits that detect the body heat of prey, all combine to make snakes the marvelous and intriguing creatures they are today.

Mouth

A snake's mouth is uniquely adapted to the type and large size of the prey that must pass through it. The bones of the lower jaw are not affixed to the skull as ours are, nor connected at the chin. Muscles and ligaments allow each side to drop down and be pushed forward, alternatingly grabbing hold of prey and pulling it further into the throat, as the other side moves forward for a new grip. Once past the jaws, the prey is moved along to the stomach by muscle contractions and S-shaped curves of the body.

Teeth. These are arranged in a single row on the bottom and two rows on top, are relatively small compared to

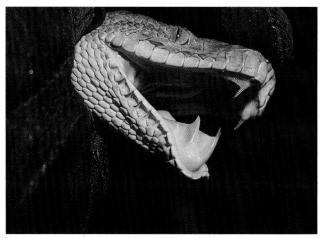

Four good reasons to think twice before buying an emerald tree boa.

most mammals, but they are needle sharp and curved inward for holding prey. The phrase "relatively small" loses its meaning as boas grow, and does not apply at all to emerald tree boas, who's unusually large canine-like teeth earned them the Latin name *Corallus caninus*. A bite from a small boa often results in two mirror-image, horseshoe-shaped rows of tiny punctures from the teeth of the top and bottom jaws, with little pain but sometimes a great deal of blood. A bite from a very large boa, however, can be very painful. Wash any snakebite thoroughly with an antibacterial soap.

A snake's elastic skin, of which the scales are only a part, stretches to allow passage of large prey during swallowing.

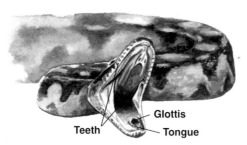

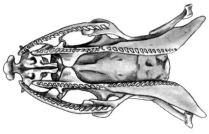

Glottis

Teeth

Tongue

The inside of a snake's mouth. Note the glottis, or windpipe, at the bottom of the mouth, which allows breathing even while swallowing large prey.

Once seized, prey animals have difficulty escaping from the rows of sharp teeth, curved toward the throat.

Windpipe. At the bottom of a snake's mouth is the opening of the glottis, or windpipe. This amazing adaptation allows the snake to extrude the windpipe past large prey while swallowing. When disturbed, some boas may open the mouth and exhale loudly, producing a very loud hissing sound as the air exits the glottis. This is the only oral sound snakes make, as they have no vocal chords. The glottis does not branch off directly to the nasal passages as in humans. The external nasal openings are connected instead to openings in the snake's palate. In cases of respiratory disease

A snake's tongue is its primary sensory tool, collecting airborne particles to be sensed and evaluated by the Jacobson's organ.

or mouth rot, mucous may plug the internal nasal openings, forcing the snake to open its mouth in order to breathe.

Tongue

The deeply forked tongue, a trademark of all snakes, is attached to the floor of the mouth in front of the windpipe. Thought by some to be a stinger of some sort, the tongue is actually quite harmless, and is the snake's primary means of identifying the objects around it. Tiny odor particles in the air are picked up by the soft, delicate tongue as it flicks in and out through a small notch in the rostral (nose) scale. Once retracted, the tongue is inserted into a depression in the roof of the mouth, the Jacobson's organ, where the particles are "tasted" and identified. Food, mates, enemies, a familiar hiding place—all can be identified with a single flick of a snake's tongue.

Sight and Sound

All boas have eyes with elliptical pupils, suited for efficient light-gathering during nocturnal foraging. Their eyes are often colored to blend in with the color or pattern of the head. Snakes do not have moveable eyelids, and therefore do not blink. Instead, each eye is covered and protected by a clear ocular scale, also referred to as the eyecap, spectacle, or brille. The eyesight is moderately good for short distances, alerting the snake to movement in its vicinity and directing an accurate strike if necessary, but it is the tongue that determines just what the object is.

Snakes have no external ears and are almost completely deaf to airborne sounds. They do, however, retain remnants of the inner ear that are sensitive to vibrations traveling through the ground, and possibly very low frequency sound waves. Think of that before placing your stereo speakers on top of your snake cage and cranking up the heavy metal. I once placed the cage of an emerald tree boa on top of a small refrigerator during a space shortage in my snake room. It wasn't until my forehead touched the glass one day that I realized the poor snake was housed in a permanent vibrator whenever the refrigerator was running!

Locomotion

Snakes owe their unequaled flexibility to the fact that their backbone consists of hundreds of vertebrae. Each vertebra is attached to a pair of ribs, and each pair of ribs controls one ventral scale. A snake can literally walk itself forward in a straight line using its ribs. More often, snakes use a combination of rib-walking and pushing coils of the body against the ground and other objects in their classic serpentine movement to get around. Snakes are awkward and uncomfortable when placed on very smooth surfaces such as glass.

Speed is rarely an issue of concern when dealing with boas. Unless agitated, boas take life at a slow, relaxed pace, another of their advantages over some of the more nervous colubrids.

A Tail with a Happy Ending

Snakes may appear to be all tail, but of course they have a head, neck,

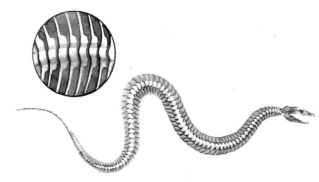

Hundreds of vertebrae and ribs give snakes their incredible flexibility.

and body, too. The tail begins at the anal vent and the cloaca, the chamber into which the digestive, urinary, and reproductive systems terminate. Unlike lizards, snakes cannot drop and regenerate their tails. Like the tongue, the harmless tip of the tail is thought by some people to be a stinger. While it is true that some

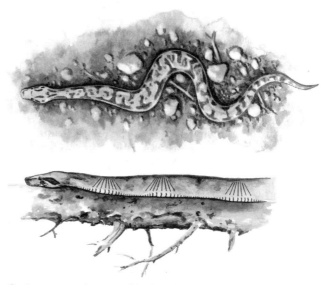

Snakes move using a combination of "walking" the ribs and pushing against stationary objects.

snakes may actually use it to poke a hand or arm when restrained, they are not even capable of breaking the skin. This particular behavior is not common in boas, many of which have relatively short, blunt tails.

Defecation and Urination

Defecation and urination occur through the cloaca at the base of the tail. Water is conserved by passing urates in a semisolid form, typically appearing as a white pasty or sandy substance, either separately or in conjunction with the passing of feces. In well-hydrated animals, a great deal of liquid may also be expelled, while dehydrated specimens may pass only solid, rock-hard balls of uric acid.

Feces contain waste products, including feathers and hair, the only part of prey animals that cannot be digested by the strong stomach acids. Boas do not defecate as often or as quickly after feeding as do colubrids, one of their advantages as pets. A boa fed weekly may only defecate once every one to three weeks. Well-formed stools are an indication of good health. Runny, foul-smelling stools, or those containing blood, mucous, or green bile, may be signs of disease or internal parasites. Consult your veterinarian if these appear.

Regular shedding of the epidermis permits growth and aids in eliminating external parasites. Young snakes shed more frequently than adults.

Growth and Shedding

Growth in boas will depend largely upon the frequency and amount of feeding. As a rule, the first two years will produce rapid growth. Some breeders overfeed juveniles in an attempt to achieve breeding size quicker, with mixed results. The outcome is more often obesity, small litter sizes, and a shortened lifespan.

All snakes need to shed their outer skin, or epidermis, as they grow. The first shed usually occurs several days after birth, and can be repeated as often as once a month for a rapidly growing juvenile. An injured snake may also proceed through several sheds in rapid succession. Adults may only shed three or four times per year.

The Shedding Process

The shedding process, or ecdysis, begins with the snake taking on a milky appearance, often most noticeable in the eyes, caused by secretions loosening the old epidermis. Colors and patterns darken and fade. Such snakes are referred to as being cloudy, opaque, or "in the blue." This condition typically lasts for a few days to a week, during which time the snake may not feed and may be irritable due to reduced vision. It is best not to handle or attempt to feed it. Provide a large water dish, however, as many snakes like to soak at this time. Remember to fill it only halfway, or you'll have an overflow when the snake curls up inside.

Two to three days before shedding, the snake's normal coloration returns. With certain exceptions, such as desert-dwelling rosy boas, low humidity can result in shedding difficulties. This is common in our artificially air-conditioned and heated indoor environments. If your snake regularly sheds in patches instead of in one piece, and will not soak in its water dish, try misting the snake and its enclosure with water once or twice daily to prepare for shedding. If you use any of the commercial plastic hide boxes, it is a good idea to mist the inside of the hide box, as well.

Shedding begins with the snake rubbing its head against cage walls, rocks, branches, and even its own body in order to pull the outer skin loose from the edge of its mouth. The skin is then peeled back over the top of the head and under the chin, turning inside-out as the snake literally crawls out of it. Often, the skin will continuously roll up as the snake crawls out, leaving a "doughnut" of shed skin when finished. If the snake is unable to get the skin off, you may have to mist it heavily, or soak it in a sink or bathtub, and work the skin off yourself, but never begin the process until the snake has started to shed on its own.

Shed skins should be checked to ensure that they include the eyecaps, the clear scales that cover the eyes. One eyecap left on may not pose a problem; the snake may rub it off later, or it may come off with the next shedding. Continued failure of the eyecaps to come off, however, could lead to infection in or around the eyes. An unshed eyecap can be dealt with by moistening it with water, then removing it with blunt tweezers if there is a piece of attached skin to grab onto, or by rubbing a finger or damp towel backwards across it while applying very gentle pressure.

After shedding, your snake's colors will be at their brightest. This is an especially good time for photography or, assuming it hasn't eaten during the shedding process, for feeding.

Longevity

Boa constrictors are some of the longest-lived species of snakes, with records in excess of 20 years being common. A boa at the Philadelphia

Snakes have no eyelids or external ears. The elliptical pupils common to all boas are clearly seen on this Hog Island boa.

Zoological Gardens lived to the very old age of 40 years! Certainly, with proper care and good luck, your boa could live 10 to 15 years or longer.

Faded color and cloudy eyes indicate this Madagascar ground boa will shed its skin in about one week.

21

HOW-TO:
Sex Determination

Boas are one of the few groups of snakes with an external feature that can often be used to accurately indicate sex. Male boas may possess spurs, claw-like remnants of their long-lost hind legs, on either side of the cloaca. In species where both males and females possess spurs, the male's are typically much larger, or, if the same size, more strongly recurved.

Probing

For species lacking spurs, or for juveniles with spurs that are just too small to be reliable, a sexing method referred to as *probing* is used. A narrow, blunt-tipped probe, lubricated with water or a nonspermicidal lubricating jelly, is inserted through the snake's cloaca and into one of two openings into the base of the tail. In males, these openings are the inverted (inside-out) *hemipenes*. In females, these are musk glands, into

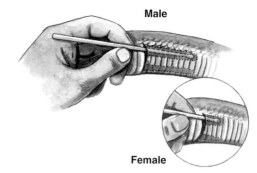

Male

Female

Step 1—Gently insert the blunt probe into one of two small openings in the base of the tail, until resistance is felt. Mark the point of deepest penetration with your thumbnail before extracting the probe.

Step 2—Hold the probe against the tail, with your thumbnail again at the vent, to determine the depth probed in terms of subcaudal scales. Average probe depth will be 2 to 5 scales for females and 7 to 12 scales for males.

which the probe should not penetrate as deeply as in the male. When resistance is felt, a thumbnail is pressed against the probe at the spot where it enters the cloaca, thereby marking the depth of the probe. By then extracting the probe and holding it along the bottom of the tail, with the thumbnail again at the cloaca, the depth of the probe in relation to subcaudal scales (the scales on the bottom of the tail) can be determined. Although it varies by species, the average probe depth will be two to five scales

for females and seven to twelve scales for males.

I strongly suggest that you let an experienced keeper guide you and demonstrate the probing technique first, and perhaps practice on a few less expensive snakes whose sex is already known. *Inserting a probe too far can cause injury or lead to infection.* The musk gland into which the probe is inserted in females is delicate and can accidentally be perforated, leading to the animal being incorrectly sexed as a male.

In species that have them, pronounced pelvic spurs are a good indication that the snake is a male. Spurs are typically shorter or absent in females.

Sexing probes. Probes are often sold in sets of various sizes, for probing very small to extremely large snakes. Seek professional guidance before attempting to probe snakes yourself.

"Popping"

Another method of sexing that works well with juveniles is "popping" the hemipenes. Again, let an experienced keeper demonstrate the technique to avoid injury to your snake. By holding the snake upside-down, a thumbnail is pressed against the bottom of the tail below the cloaca, and then pushed upward toward the cloaca. The other thumb, pressed against the belly just above the cloaca, bends the snake slightly backward and pulls the vent open. If done correctly, in a male, one or both hemipenes will evert, or turn rightside-out, from the inside of the tail. This method can prove a male beyond a shadow of a doubt, but a "female" might just

"Popping," or manually everting the hemipenes, can be useful in sexing juveniles. This method should also be demonstrated by a professional before attempting it yourself.

be a male that will not evert. Many breeders master this technique well enough to trust their judgment, but if in doubt, confirm a female by probing. Raising a pair of boas for years in preparation for breeding, only to find they're both males, could be frustrating.

Although most snakes purchased from professional breeders and reputable reptile pet shops will be accurately sexed, mistakes have been known to happen. If you are purchasing juveniles for future breeding projects, consider probing your animals again once you become comfortable with the procedure, especially if the size of the spurs do not support the original determination of gender.

Interpreting Behavioral Clues

Snakes cannot talk. That is obvious. But there is a lot they can tell you by their actions. Even breeders with large collections come to recognize, and even expect, certain behaviors and preferences of individual animals. Given the chance, your boa might just tell you what it is that it needs. Perhaps the most obvious clue is temperature preference. If you have provided a temperature gradient in the cage, and your snake continuously remains at the warm end, it may not be warm enough. If the snake remains at the cool end, the cage is too hot.

A boa curled up in a water dish is not uncommon. But what if it stays in the dish for days, or has never before been seen soaking? Your records and the snake's appearance may indicate that it is shedding time. If a hide box has not been provided, your snake may be using the dish as a hiding place. Check the bottom of the dish closely for drowned mites. Heavy infestations of these tiny bloodsucking parasites can drive a snake into the water for relief. High temperatures, and possibly even constipation, may be other reasons for soaking. Consider all the possibilities. Note that some rainbow boas may be habitual soakers, but this species has a high resistance to blister disease and prolonged soaking is less of a concern.

Getting to know your boa's habits can tell you many things. For instance, a well-fed boa will often stay quietly curled in its hide box, with just the head poking out—an endearing habit compared to other snakes that stay completely hidden. When I don't see a head for two or three days, it's time to investigate, usually confirming my suspicion that the snake is preparing to shed. A snake cruising the cage tells me it is ready to eat, while one curled up uncharacteristically at the opposite end of the cage may be indicating that it left me a present under the hide box. Now there's gratitude for you.

Observation is the key to early detection of some diseases. Lethargy, uncoordination, respiratory distress, or refusing to feed may require closer scrutiny. A boa that continuously points its nose straight up may be suffering from a neurological disorder known as "star-gazer's disease" (see page 60). Early detection and immediate quarantine of suspected problems is essential. If you keep more than one snake, interpreting behavioral clues could save your entire collection.

Caging

Selecting a Cage

The only perfect cage is the one that satisfies all your needs and those of your boa. Typically, your final choice will be a compromise but a number of factors must be considered:

- What type of boa?
- How big will it grow?
- How much do you want to spend?
- How much room do you have available?
- How many cages will you need?
- Does it need to be appealing to the eye, or just functional?

For a single snake or a very small collection, large attractive cages will do much to enhance your enjoyment of the hobby. Give your snake as much room as you can afford to, physically and financially. Constantly upgrading cage space can get expensive. Looking to the future and your boa's adult size will save you money later on.

A good rule of thumb for cage space is to select a cage that is two-thirds the length of the snake. A 2-foot (.6 m) cage is adequate for rosy and sand boas, 3 to 4 feet (.9–1.2 m) for rainbow boas, and 4 to 6 feet (1.2–1.8 m) long for most boa constrictors. Most boas are great climbers, and heavy branches allow them to make good use of vertical space. Arboreal species such as tree boas will require tall enclosures with a number of branches or perches.

Cage height for non-arboreal species in a large or growing collection may have to be sacrificed to allow for stackable or shelved units. A number of companies now produce affordable cages and multi-cage units specifically designed for reptiles, made out of easily cleaned materials such as glass, plastic, and melamine (laminated fiberboard). Available options, besides size and materials, may include door types, litter dams (see page 27), vent sizes, and pre-wired heating elements.

Glass Aquarium

The most common cage used by beginners is the glass aquarium with a screen top. The small, ground-dwelling rosy and sand boas could live their entire lives in a 10-gallon (38 L) aquarium. If you have the space, I have always preferred the 20-gallon (76 L) size, especially if a lamp or other

Large snakes need large enclosures. The snake is an adult Dumeril's boa.

Building Your Own Cage

If you like to build things, you might want to build your own cage. The interior will need to be water resistant and impervious to spills and high humidity. Silicon aquarium sealant should be used to seal all joints. Exposed, untreated wood should be avoided for the interior of cages, as it will absorb water and feces. When soiled, untreated wood is nearly impossible to clean and disinfect completely, resulting in bacterial growth. Uncovered peg-board or fiberboard may be weakened when wet, to the point of allowing a snake to push right through. If you intend to use newspaper as substrate, considering the size of your local paper when drawing up plans can save folding, cutting or wasting paper later.

Doors

Front opening cages allow you to keep several cages in a vertical space, usually not actually stacked but shelved in a way that allows for lights to be placed on top. If high humidity is important, select or build a cage with small vent openings on the back or sides, and only minimal screening on top for lighting. Doors can be one of several types—single sliding glass, two-piece sliding glass bypass, single-hinged swingout, two-door hinged swingout, or hinged dropdown. A single sliding door of glass or Lexan offers great visibility, but requires clearance on either side to open the door, and cannot be fully opened. Bypass doors allow access to only half the cage at a time, a problem when a big boa decides it doesn't want to come out or go back inside. Hinged doors typically have a frame that reduces the view, but allows the cage to be opened fully for ease of access to your snake or for cleaning.

Latches

Regardless of the type of doors, secure latches or pins are required to

A simple, yet functional and attractive cage setup for large boas. Climbing branches must be secured to prevent tipping. Fiberglass heating pad bolted to underside of bench provides heat to snakes resting above and below.

heating device is to be used at one end. Screen tops allow for excellent ventilation for these dry-habitat species, although stacking is impossible and lights must be removed to open the lid. Another major drawback of screen tops is the absence or ineffectiveness of latching mechanisms. If a snug and secure top can be found, all boas can start off in such an aquarium, but few can stay in one for very long.

Multi-cage unit for medium-sized boas. Professionally built and well-lit cages make a handsome addition to any room.

keep your snake inside. Don't trust a tight fit or the weight of sliding glass to prevent escapes. Boas are strong and heavy, and they will get out. A thin rubber wedge firmly inserted between the overlap of sliding glass doors will help prevent them from being pushed open by your snakes. Where both snakes and children are present, a locking mechanism will protect each from the other.

For cages having doors that extend to the floor, a litter dam is a useful feature. Litter dams—short barriers across the front of the cage just behind the doors—prevent substrate, feces, and spilled water from getting into door tracks or spilling out when the cage is opened.

Manufacturers of vacuum-formed plastic cages are able to offer seamless enclosures with rounded corners and edges, thereby eliminating the crevices where liquid, bacteria, and mites can cause problems. These cages are also very lightweight.

Rack Systems

For large numbers of adult rosy or sand boas, or juveniles of almost any species, nothing beats the simplicity of a rack system. A rack is nothing more than a set of shelves, typically constructed of moisture-resistant melamine or laminated wood, with each shelf holding one or more plastic storage boxes. By having the shelves built to the exact height and slightly deeper than the depth of the boxes to be used, each shelf acts as the lid to the boxes below. A backing is required to prevent boxes from being pushed in too far. Pegboard makes a good backing and increases ventilation. Shelves must be built to exact tolerances—too loose and snakes may escape or strangle, too tight and the boxes stick.

Types of Boxes

Various suitable boxes are available, some rigid and clear, others flexible

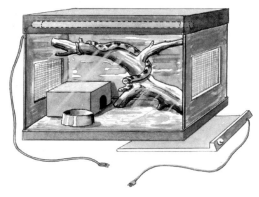

Basic cage setup for small to medium boas, with hide box, water dish, climbing branch, light fixture, and heating pad underneath. The hide box and water dish should always be at the cool end of the cage.

and opaque. Flexible Rubbermaid and Sterilite brand storage boxes in several sizes (shoe, sweater, blanket, etc.) can be found at discount and department stores (watch for sales after Christmas). Think hard about your future needs before you start building or buying racks and boxes. I prefer the less-expensive Sterilite boxes in 15- and 32-quart (14–30 L) sizes. Because these boxes are the same height, racks are built wide enough to hold three 15-quart (14 L) and deep

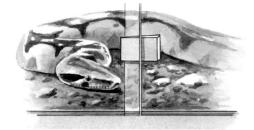

A thin rubber wedge firmly inserted between sliding glass doors will help prevent snakes from pushing them open. A more reliable locking mechanism is recommended when large boa constrictors or children are involved.

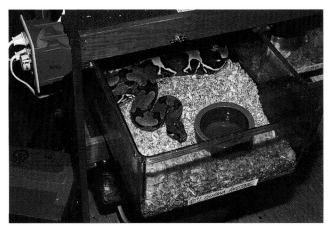

A sophisticated rack system used for breeding snakes at Glades Herp, a reptile store.

Ventilation

Ventilation is provided by drilling or burning a large quantity of airholes into all four sides of each box. Don't skimp on holes, particularly when housing low-humidity species. Burning holes with a soldering iron is quicker, makes smoother holes, and nearly eliminates the cracking and shattering that can occur from drilling. Heating for the unit can be provided by running heat tape or routering a groove for a heating cable across each shelf, 3 to 4 inches (8–10 cm) from the back. By cutting an opening at each end of the shelf, the heating element can be snaked (no pun intended) from shelf to shelf, and even from rack to rack, all connected to a timer and/or thermostat for temperature control. Side or back lighting is possible, but most rack users rely solely on ambient light from the front.

Maintenance

Maintenance using this type of system is quick and easy: slide a box out

enough for two 32-quart (30 L) boxes per shelf. Rack units should not be built much wider than this, as the units are extremely heavy and shelves will sag in the middle. Wheels are highly recommended for ease of movement.

Rack system suitable for housing large numbers of juveniles, or small boas such as rosy and sand boas. Additional heat can be provided by using heating cable.

One or more rack systems can be heated by a single heating cable, recessed into a groove along each shelf and attached to a rheostat for subtle adjustment of temperature levels. Follow manufacturer guidelines carefully when using any electrical device.

part-way, replace the water dish and newspaper or other substrate, and slide the box back in. My rule is that if feces touch the plastic, the box must either be washed and disinfected or replaced. So long as care is exercised in pushing boxes in, racks are virtually escape-proof. The lack of screen prevents active or nervous snakes from rubbing the nose raw. Check the underside of shelves from time to time during cleaning, as mold or mildew can result from inadequate ventilation.

Substrate

Though not the most attractive or naturalistic material, newspaper is by far the best substrate for large boas. Newspaper is inexpensive and plentiful (I have my substrate delivered to my driveway every day), and unlike other materials such as gravel or wood chips, it can easily be completely discarded and replaced after every defecation or water spill, no matter how small. Failure to adequately clean and disinfect cages is one of the primary causes of health problems in snakes.

Some keepers maintain small boas on sand, gravel, or wood shavings. One possible drawback is the occasional ingestion of such substrate during feeding. In small amounts, this usually poses no problem, but impaction and blockage of the digestive tract is possible. As with any substrate, complete removal of soiled areas or water spills is required to prevent bacteria or mold buildup.

Cedar wood should never be used in snake enclosures, either as a substrate or in hiding places, because of its irritating fumes.

Temperature

Proper temperature is one of the most important factors involved in maintaining good health in all reptiles. With a few exceptions, boas are tropical species adapted to very warm temper-atures. Without sufficient heat, adequate digestion and disease resistance cannot be maintained.

Providing a temperature gradient or a warm basking area in your cage through the use of a heat lamp, heat tape, or heating pad at one end will allow your boa to choose the best temperature for its needs. Under-cage heaters should warm only one-third to one-half of the enclosure. The warm end or basking area should be at the high end of the snake's preferred range, around 85–92°F (29–33°C) for most tropical boas, with the remainder of the cage in the low 80s F (27–29°C). A drop of several degrees at night is recommended.

Regardless of the heating element used, care must be exercised to avoid overheating the cage, burning the snake, or burning your house down. Always follow manufacturer instructions for safe use. Before returning any

Two types of plastic cages produced by Neodesha Plastics.

snakes to the cage, check temperatures carefully after the heat has been on for one to two hours. A rheostat or thermostat may be required to more accurately adjust the heat to the desired level. Incandescent light bulbs can get extremely hot, and must be placed outside the cage and separated by screening so that the snake cannot touch it. Make sure the fixture is secure, well ventilated, and away from combustible materials such as paper or curtains.

Optimally, the snake will spend most of its time somewhere in the middle of the cage, indicating that a preferred mid-range temperature has been selected. If your snake spends all of its time at the warm end, the cage may be too cool. Likewise, if your snake stays at the cool end, the cage may be too warm. Before making adjustments, however, consider other factors that may also be involved. For a secretive snake, security may take priority over comfort. During daylight hours, a secretive boa may choose to remain in its hide box, even though it would be more comfortable in the warm zone. For such a snake, non-light-emitting heat sources, such as ceramic heat fixtures, heat tape, or heating pads, may be left on overnight.

If you're one of those cold-blooded types who keep their homes warm at all times, or if you keep your collection in a temperature-controlled room, then it is possible to maintain boas without providing additional heat. Generally, boas should spend at least several hours a day in the low to mid-80s F (27–29°C). A nighttime drop of several degrees is acceptable and even natural, but except during brumation in preparation for breeding, and especially after feeding, prolonged exposure to temperatures below 80°F (27°C) should be avoided.

Observation and knowing your snake's habits can help you determine if your cage temperature is adequate. Regurgitation may indicate that the environment is too cold; uncharacteristic soaking in the water dish may be an indication that it is too warm.

Lighting and Photoperiod

Although it is currently accepted that snakes do not require full-spectrum lights like other reptiles, many keepers still use them, both for their color quality and for the more natural ultraviolet light produced. After all, who knows just what benefits are being lost when we take sun-loving creatures out of the sun?

Regardless of the source, snakes should be provided with a daily cycle, or photoperiod, of light and darkness. Lights should never be left on 24 hours a day. If enough ambient light is present from windows or skylights, no additional light is needed, and the natural photoperiod of day and night is sufficient.

Additional cage lighting can be in the form of incandescent or fluorescent bulbs, connected to a timer to regulate photoperiod. Photoperiod can be a constant 12 hours on and 12 off, or it can be changed occasionally to match the natural seasonal fluctuations of day and night. Prior to and during winter brumation in preparation for breeding, many breeders will reduce daylight hours, imitating the shorter days of winter as part of their seasonal breeding cues.

Humidity

The most common humidity-related problem seen in snakes is dry skin and poor shedding. Even in regions where high humidity is the norm outdoors, air conditioning and heating can dry out the environment indoors. Drafty conditions accelerate the drying process. This problem can usually be avoided by providing a water dish or pool large enough for the snake to soak in. A large dish or pool also serves to increase cage humidity through evaporation. If the snake continues to have problems, or spends too much time soaking, reduce the amount of ventilation to further increase the humidity. A daily misting of the snake and its enclosure may be required. Do not soak the cage and substrate, or overly restrict ventilation, as mold and fungus may result. Room humidifiers are also an option, if all species in the room need higher humidity. A very helpful tip is to use distilled or spring water in humidifiers and misting bottles as calcium and lime deposits in tap water will quickly encrust humidifier heating elements and cage glass.

Rainbow boas and emerald tree boas are known to require high humidity. I use large water dishes and smaller ventilation openings for my rainbow boas, and only mist them just before shedding, although one juvenile did require daily mistings during his first year. Due to the increased risk of mold and fungus from damp cages, I suggest letting each snake's actions, skin appearance, and shedding results determine whether daily misting is needed. Unless you live in an area of consistently high humidity, emerald tree boas will likely require daily mistings. This species of boa should be kept only by serious, dedicated herpetoculturists.

For sand boas and rosy boas, high humidity is not only unnecessary, but detrimental. For these species, small water dishes and excellent ventilation are a must. Some keepers only offer water to these boas once or twice a week, removing the water dish after the snake has had an opportunity to drink. I prefer good ventilation and leaving the water dish in the cage.

Most electronics and hardware stores carry a variety of combination digital thermometers and hygrometers for simultaneous monitoring of temperature and humidity.

Cleaning and Disinfecting

Assuming you have acquired parasite and disease-free snakes, failure to maintain a clean enclosure is perhaps the number one cause of serious problems in captive snakes. The inability to distance itself from feces means the snake is exposed to higher concentrations of bacteria than would be encountered in the wild. In high enough concentrations, or when combined with a weakened immune system resulting from disease or suboptimum cage temperatures, such bacteria can quickly overwhelm the snake's natural defenses. Simply replacing wet or soiled substrate is not enough. A snake crawling through excrement will spread it wherever he crawls—through the water dish, over the hide box, up the glass. What you can't see can still hurt your snake.

The best way to clean a cage thoroughly is to remove the snake and discard any disposable substrate or hide box. The enclosure and all reusable objects such as the water dish, plastic hide box, or perches should be washed in hot, soapy water, then disinfected with a bleach or other disinfectant solution, and allowed to air dry. Some cleaning solutions such as Roccal-D are also virucidal, giving an added protection against disease, but they can be very expensive. A solution of warm, soapy water (liquid dish soap) and bleach (1 teaspoon per gallon) makes an effective yet inexpensive disinfectant. Consult with your veterinarian if you are concerned about which is best for you to use. Always follow product instructions and warnings and your vet's advice. Too much of a good thing or misuse can have disastrous results, for you and your boas.

If you only wish to clean a portion of the cage, do not spray cleaning fluids inside with the snake or water dish present. Instead, spray onto a paper

Arboreal snakes, like this Amazon tree boa, do best in tall cages with numerous branches.

haps to achieve the true purpose of keeping these pets in our homes—to bring nature into our unnatural human habitats. Unfortunately, most boas are just too large for such lushly planted vivaria. The focus for boa enclosures should be on simplicity, functionality, and ease of maintenance.

The Hide Box

A hide box is an important cage component and should generally be placed at the darker or cooler end of the enclosure. Large boa constrictors seem content to remain in the open more than juveniles, perhaps because in the wild they have few enemies at this size and just as few places large enough to hide in. But even boas that ordinarily spend little time in the hide box may utilize it while opaque, after eating, or if stressed. Types of suitable hiding places are limited only by your imagination. Any object that provides a dark, snug fit will suffice. If one is not provided, snakes will typically hide under the substrate. The entrance to the box should be large enough for the snake to crawl through after a big meal. For small boas, any empty household cardboard box can be used, including shoe, cereal, or bathroom tissue boxes. Avoid boxes with strong odors, or ones that formerly contained substances that could be harmful to your snake, such as laundry detergent. Durable commercially produced plastic hide boxes are available in various sizes and colors, and can be washed and reused as needed. Faux stone caves, though strong and attractive, can be difficult to clean thoroughly when defecated on. For very large boas, inverted rubber or plastic tubs with an entrance hole cut out make good, strong hiding places.

towel or rag well away from the cage and then wipe the inside of the enclosure. Good ventilation is a must.

Making Your Boa Feel at Home

Many herpetoculturists are turning to naturalistic vivaria these days to enhance the life of their pets, and per-

Almost any cardboard box makes a suitable hide box. Commercially produced plastic hide boxes are washable and durable.

Branches or Perches

A strong branch or perch will allow your boa to exercise its climbing instincts, while utilizing the vertical space of the cage. Besides, it's fun to watch snakes climb. For very large boa constrictors in equally large enclosures, many keepers provide a bench or ledge for their snakes to lie on, sometimes even attaching heating pads to the underside, providing heat above and below the bench. One labor-saving technique is to use perches or benches securely attached only to the sides of the enclosure instead of resting on the floor. When cleaning is required, the snake is often up out of the way and does not need to be moved while the floor substrate is replaced. Be sure that when heavy branches, benches, or rocks are used, it is impossible for them to collapse or fall onto your snake.

Provide a water dish large enough for drinking and for soaking.

Water Dishes

A water dish large enough to soak in is a necessity. Snakes drink by submerging and repeatedly dropping the lower jaw, drawing water into the mouth and throat. The water dish should be replaced and washed twice a week, or whenever any foreign matter is observed in it; it is not unusual for snakes to defecate in the water dish.

Feeding

What They Eat and How Often

All snakes are strictly carnivorous. For most boas, the preferred foods are rodents, other small mammals, and birds. Juveniles and some small species of boas may consume lizards or frogs, either occasionally or exclusively (refer to the species accounts beginning on page 63 for food preferences). Such a whole-animal diet provides all the vitamins and minerals required for growth and good health. Additional vitamin supplements are not needed, even for growing juveniles.

Opportunistic feeders in the wild, snakes are capable of swallowing extremely large sizes and quantities of prey when the chance presents itself, and going long periods without food during lean times. As pets, it is better for them to be fed moderate amounts on a regular basis. Active or growing boas should be fed about once a week. One food animal of appropriate size to put a small bulge in the snake's stomach will suffice, or feed two if faster growth is desired. Large boa constrictors feeding on jumbo rats or rabbits, and less active species such as emerald tree boas, should be fed once every two to four weeks. Two smaller food animals are preferable over one larger one. Because prey items are swallowed whole, digestion is a slow process. Especially under suboptimum temperatures, a prey item that is too large may actually turn rancid inside the stomach and be regurgitated.

Chicken and other fowl are readily accepted by many boas; however, a diet of chicken often results in soft, foul-smelling stools. Uncooked chicken can also be a source of *Salmonella* bacteria. Most keepers will feed chicken only as a last resort for difficult feeders, or on newly imported specimens.

Your snake will tell you when it is hungry by exploring its cage. Don't be too quick to accommodate it, though. Snakes in the wild must search days and even weeks for a meal. The exercise will do your boa good, preventing problems such as obesity or constipation that can result from overfeeding. An obese snake has a body that appears disproportionately large compared to the head. Skin showing between rows of scales may give a striped appearance. Rosy boas in particular, being adapted to a hard desert life, are known to turn excess food into fat rather than just faster growth. A rosy boa with a lumpy appearance should have its food intake reduced.

Constricting

Mention the word constrictor to most non-herpetoculturists and the image that pops into mind is of huge boa constrictors crushing people and prey to death. Although boa constrictors are aptly named, all species of boas are constrictors, as are most other snakes that must subdue potentially dangerous prey. Pythons, rat snakes, and kingsnakes are also constrictors. Snakes that are not constrictors often depend on venom to dispatch dangerous prey, or feed on relatively harmless prey such as fish, frogs, insects, or worms.

Despite the fact that boas are indeed very powerful constrictors, the "bone-crushing" reputation is undeserved. Not only do they not break any bones while constricting prey, even a fairly large specimen can exert little more than a hearty hug around the abdomen of an average adult human. Care must be exercised, however, not to place boas longer than 6 feet (2 m) around the neck or leave them unsupervised with small children. Having an extra person around when handling snakes longer than 8 feet (2.4 m) is recommended. Constricting behavior while being handled is usually caused by the snake's fear of falling. If your boa becomes frightened and begins to constrict, remain calm and, beginning at the head or tail, unwrap it like a scarf.

To constrict its prey, a snake first grabs the animal with its sharp teeth, then quickly wraps one or more coils around it. The powerful coils are tightened whenever the prey exhales or relaxes its muscles, making it impossible for the prey to breathe. Death results fairly quickly from asphyxiation and the pressure exerted on the heart and circulatory system. When the prey has been dispatched, the snake relaxes its coils and begins swallowing. If the prey was not originally grabbed by the head, the snake may release it and search for the head, or simply walk its jaws along the prey until the nose is found. Prey swallowed head first will obviously go down much easier than if swallowed backwards, but don't be surprised or concerned if your boa occasionally forgets this. I once watched an Argentine boa constrictor consume a large rat sideways, folding it into a U-shape that seemed impossibly too wide to swallow. The truth is, there is very little those elastic jaws can't handle, and little that you can do to change things once swallowing has begun. If you can't bear to watch, don't.

When consuming exceptionally large prey, it is not unusual for boas to utilize their constricting capabilities to aid in swallowing. After swallowing begins, a single coil is thrown around the prey just in front of the snake's nose. As the prey is pulled through the coil by the snake's jaws, it is compressed and stretched to its full length. Again, no bones are being broken in the process.

After eating, it is perfectly normal for a snake to "yawn," as it moves its jaws back into place. Rubbing its mouth on the cage or cage accessories is also common.

Live, Fresh-Killed, or Frozen?

Frozen rodents have a number of advantages over live prey. Live mice and rats have been known to severely injure and kill snakes—even large boas and pythons if they refuse to eat the prey—and must never be allowed to remain in the cage unobserved. Even in a powerful constrictor's coils, a feisty prey animal can take out the snake's eye with one quick bite. Why take the chance, when frozen-thawed rodents are readily accepted by most snakes? Frozen rodents are also convenient and less expensive than live ones purchased in a pet shop, and freezing can reduce or eliminate parasites in food animals. A freezer full of appropriate-sized rodents ensures that when you're ready to feed them, each snake will get the correct type and size of food needed. Just be careful about letting your house guests go snooping through your freezer!

If you do not have a reptile store or exotic pet shop nearby that offers frozen rodents, suppliers can be found in the classified ads of reptile magazines. Pricing is often based on the quantity ordered, so order up to a six-month supply or combine orders with other snake-keeping friends. Include expected off-feed periods such as shedding or brumation when calculating future needs. Frozen rodents are typically shipped by overnight carrier, packed in insulating styrofoam. If available, request that dry ice be included,

Madagascar ground boa dispatching prey by constriction.

Young mice and rats, referred to as "pinkies," "fuzzies," or "crawlers," which have not yet developed sharp teeth, can safely be offered alive to smaller boas and even left in the cage overnight. For boas that need a larger meal, the safest alternative is to use stunned or freshly killed rodents instead. The most common stunning method is to grasp the rodent by the tail, swing it in an arc, and strike the back of its head sharply against a board or other hard object. A stunned rodent can recover, so keep your eye on it. Hopefully, dispatching rodents yourself will only be a temporary requirement, as the goal should be to get your snake switched over to frozen-thawed prey.

especially if your order is all small rodents or if the amount you ordered does not completely fill the shipping container.

Emerald tree boas ambush and swallow prey while hanging from a branch.

Converting from Live to Frozen Prey

In a perfect world, every snake would relish frozen-thawed prey. However, it's not a perfect world, and some snakes simply will not eat rodents that have been frozen, but with a bit of ingenuity, time, and patience, you can probably get your snake converted to frozen prey.

If your boa is in good health, offer only frozen-thawed food for several weeks. Try rodents of different types, sizes, and colors, offered both during the day and at night. If a defensive snake can be antagonized into striking at a frozen rodent, it may decide to hold on and eat it. A slightly warm rodent placed in the cage after dark and left overnight often gets good results.

If the snake has not eaten in several weeks, or if you feel its health requires that it eat, then try a stunned or freshly killed rodent, or even a live one if necessary. Once a snake is in a feeding mode and the cage is filled with the right scents, you'll find it much easier to slip something by it. Have a frozen-thawed rodent ready for a bait-and-switch or for a second course. If you can get the snake to strike at the fresh prey and grab the frozen-thawed, great. If the snake gets the fresh prey, try slipping the frozen-thawed prey into its coils, too, or lay it down next to the snake, and see if it will eat both.

For those snakes that seem to recognize and refuse frozen prey, it may still be possible to mix fresh and frozen prey. As the snake finishes swallowing the fresh prey, hold the head of the frozen prey against the rump of the first. Chances are good that the snake will continue swallowing as if it were just one long rodent. Don't give up. With each feeding, try frozen prey first. Your boa may just surprise you and switch one day. Once a snake begins eating frozen prey, don't go back to live unless absolutely necessary.

Offering Food

It is always amazing to me how quickly a snake that never bites defensively can determine that an approaching object is food. One flick of the tongue is usually all it takes, with a lightning-fast strike following in just a fraction of a second. A feeding strike can be more dangerous to a keeper than a defensive strike, because the snake intends to hold on. If you've been handling rodents, or if you have some alive or thawing in the same room, don't stick your hand in a cage. Even from across the room, your snake's sensitive tongue will be able to detect the odor. Of course, you don't want to feed your snake in a dirty cage, so complete your daily cage inspection and cleaning before bringing rodents into the same room.

Using Live Prey

If you plan to feed live mice or rats purchased at a pet shop, the first thing to remember is that they like to start chewing through the bag or "critter carrier" cardboard box the moment they're put into it. They're also speedy

Four common mouse sizes for feeding snakes: pinky, fuzzy, hopper, and adult.

runners and gifted high-jumpers—if any escape, you'll have a merry chase on your hands. One mouse in my bedroom eluded capture for three days, despite being spotted and even cornered several times! So, if you have a long drive home from the pet shop, take along a deep bucket. If not, have one ready when you get home into which you can dump the rodents. This also makes it easier to select the right size if you've bought several, and easier to grab hold of their tails. Make sure the snake is away from the cage door, and toss the rodent inside. Always keep an eye on the situation until you're sure the snake has dispatched his prey.

HOW-TO:
Raising Your Own Rodents

Although the number of rodent suppliers is growing quickly, sometimes offering frozen rodents at prices 50 to 90 percent cheaper than live ones purchased at a pet shop, there are reasons that you may wish to breed your own. Snake breeders concerned about the quality and health of food items, or having large numbers of offspring to feed, may find it advantageous to maintain their own rodent breeding colony. So, too, will owners whose animals will only accept live prey. Having a rodent colony might appear at first to offer "free" food, but breeding rodents is not without its own expenses and drawbacks.

Drawbacks

Before we get into the specifics of constructing a rodent colony, let's make sure you understand what you're getting into. Unlike the fairly odorless and low maintenance characteristics of your snake, rodents are

A good ratio for a small breeding colony is one male to three or four females. The male is on the right; the female is on the left.

Two possible cage setups for raising rodents. Placing food in the top, as shown in the small cage, saves money by reducing waste.

smelly creatures that can rarely be left for more than a day or two without being tended. What will you do if you go on vacation? Mice and rats generally keep themselves quite clean, but the odor of their urine is something that will soon permeate the entire building in which they are kept. A complete change of substrate, along with scrubbing the cage, is necessary on a weekly basis to adequately control odor. I have known snake breeders who spend more time dealing with their rodents than with their snakes! To choose the best location for your colony, you will have to consider temperature as well as odor dispersal. Rodents fare and breed best when maintained at a temperature of 70–80°F (21–27°C). At higher temperatures, breeding activity decreases and urine output increases.

Expenses

Besides start-up expenses, expenditures for food, substrate, and equipment replacement will be continuous. Food can consist of high-protein dry dog food, or the more expensive but nutritionally balanced laboratory rodent chow. Pine shavings purchased in tightly packed bales

make an economical substrate. Always buy in bulk for savings. As for equipment, rodents are notorious for gnawing everything in sight, including water bottles. If the apparatus is to be placed inside the cage, glass bottles with metal supports and tubes will hold up better than plastic.

Cages and Accessories for Rodents

Choosing cages and accessories for your rodent colony will depend on the number of rodents you wish to breed. If all you need is a few live mouse pinkies or rat pups, a single breeding group of one male and three to four females can be set up in a standard glass aquarium. The 10-gallon (38 L) size is appropriate for mice, while the 20-gallon (76 L) size can house the much larger rats. Having an extra aquarium available makes complete cage changes a snap. The clean cage can be prepared with pine shavings, and the water bottle and other cage accessories transferred, before moving the rodents themselves. When litters of pinkies must be moved, scoop the whole batch up with a paper cup or other makeshift scoop and deposit them in the same location of the new cage. Although rodents require nothing more than absorbent substrate, a water bottle, and food, they do enjoy and make regular use of hiding places, and will typically choose such secluded sites exclusively when giving birth. For a colony consisting of only a few breeding groups, I prefer to provide hard plastic hide boxes and perhaps a section of hard plastic tubing for a little variety. This would be an unnecessary burden in an extensive colony. When choosing a water bottle, select a large size with a metal hanger that hooks securely over the cage rim. Forget the cheaper suction cup bottle holders and spend your money wisely the first time. Rodents will not only chew them, but they rarely hold a full bottle for long, especially when the weight of a climbing rodent is added. Rodents are curious animals and excellent climbers, so a secure lid is as important for them as for your snakes.

Trays

For breeding a large quantity of rodents, a rack system of sliding trays is generally used. Heavy-duty rubber or plastic trays such as those used in the restaurant industry for dirty dishes are ideal. Trays should have only rounded corners and edges inside, with no angles or depressions that can be chewed. Most breeders build their own rack systems out of lumber and heavy wire. A simple design is to use 2 inch × 4 inch (5 cm × 122 cm) lumber to create a frame, with smaller strips of wood attached in pairs at regular intervals along the inner

sides so as to create slots into which the lip of the trays can slide. Heavy wire mesh can be cut and bent to fit over each tray so as to be pulled out along with the tray. Pockets can be created in the wire in which the water bottle and food can be placed. Forcing your rodents to eat their food through the wire will save you money, preventing them from hiding it throughout the tray where it goes to waste. If space is not at an absolute premium, leave enough distance between trays to allow visual inspection through the screen without having to pull the tray out. If you're not the do-it-yourself type when it comes to building things, check with local rodent suppliers to see if they have any new or used racks for sale. If you find any, make sure that spare trays of the size the rack is designed to hold can be purchased at the same time, or at least are still available from other sources. Again, having spare trays into which you can transfer rodents saves steps and time in the cleaning process.

Litters

Female mice and rats produce average litters of six to ten young each month, and may remain fertile for eight to twelve months or longer. Breeding occurs again very soon after having a litter. The female grows extremely large in girth during the last four to five days of pregnancy. They are social animals, and will often deposit their young together in communal nests. When disturbed, the entire group, including the male, may pick up

Rack built for holding multiple trays of mice or rats.

pinkies in their mouths in an attempt to relocate them. Occasionally, the young may be eaten, especially when, through accident or oversight, food or water is not available. The young grow quickly, achieving independent "hopper" size within three to four weeks, at which stage they can be moved out to a separate grow-out cage if needed.

Mice are less accommodating than rats to new arrivals into the colony. Some breeders apply baby powder or Vick's Vap-O-Rub to the colony and the new arrival so that all members smell alike.

Breeding rodents is not for everybody. The time and extra effort involved, combined with the odor and high maintenance requirements, can easily negate the advantages inherent in having snakes as pets. However, if you find yourself constantly dealing with food supply inadequacies or shortages, it is an option you may want to consider.

Using Frozen Prey

For my collection, I order frozen rodents in bulk—never more than I can use in six months. On the day before feeding, I calculate the number of each size required, pull them from the freezer and place them in a refrigerator to thaw slowly. On feeding day, the thawed rodents are spread out under spotlights to slightly warm them before feeding. Never feed a frozen rodent that has not been completely thawed, but also avoid thawing out too fast or overheating. The latter may result in rodents breaking open during feeding—very unpleasant! Once warmed to at least room temperature, the food is offered with forceps to each snake.

Forceps

For feeding frozen-thawed food, a long set of forceps is an indispensable tool. Offering food by hand is just an invitation to be bitten. Some snakes will take the food from the forceps, while others merely like the food dropped where they can take it at their leisure. For boas over 6 feet (2 m), it is safer to simply leave the food in the cage for the snake to find.

Uneaten Food

Transferring uneaten food to other snakes carries the risk of transferring

When offering frozen-thawed prey, the tips of the forceps should not extend beyond the prey item's head, to prevent injuring the snake's mouth when it strikes.

parasites, bacteria, and disease. With some collections valued in six-digit figures, throwing away a few perfectly good rodents is well worth the precaution. If you cannot convince yourself to throw away food, at the very least refrain from reusing any rodent from a cage with a sick snake or new arrival, or if the snake's mouth was on it.

Convincing a Difficult Feeder

Nothing in herpetoculture is quite so frustrating as a snake that acts hungry, but refuses to eat. I've actually watched snakes push frozen-thawed rodents around with their nose, as if thinking, "I smell it—maybe it's under this thing." It's enough to make a grown herpeteculturist cry, but in this hobby, patience is indeed a virtue. There are some short-term circumstances under which your snake may stop feeding, and all you need to do is wait them out:

• Snakes often will not eat during their opaque period prior to shedding their skin.

• During breeding season, males may be more interested in mating than eating, even males you may consider too young to breed.

• Your snake may sense that it is winter, even if you have made the effort to keep the cage within a consistent temperature range.

If your snake is healthy, these short fasts should not be a cause for alarm. There are other possibilities, however, that will require action on your part.

The first steps in getting a difficult feeder to eat have nothing to do with food. Number one, examine the snake closely for indications of health problems or parasites that may be affecting its appetite, and consult with a qualified reptile veterinarian if you suspect that something is wrong. Next, consider the snake's enclosure. Is it warm enough? Cool temperatures can keep a snake from eating, and can cause health problems if it does eat. Is the snake stressed? Keep handling to a minimum and be sure to provide a suitable hide box. New snakes should be given time to acclimate to their new home before feeding is attempted.

If the snake appears healthy and the cage conditions are adequate, offer frozen-thawed food of different types and sizes as described in the previous section for converting snakes to frozen prey (pages 36–37), progressing to stunned, freshly killed, or live prey as required.

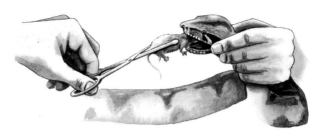

Force-feeding may be required as a last resort for snakes that refuse to eat. Gently force the dead prey item partially into the throat, and release slowly. Be patient and prepared to try again.

Force-feeding

Force-feeding should be a last resort. With the snake resting on the floor of its cage or other level surface, grasp it firmly behind the head. With the other hand, force the nose of the food item into the snake's mouth and partially into the throat. Very slowly, release your hold on the snake, and try not to move. It may take a number of tries, but hopefully the snake will finally decide to swallow the food.

Neonates can be force-fed parts of food animals, such as mouse tails or skinned chick legs; however, because of their small size, neonates could be injured during the strong restraint required for force-feeding. An alternative is to use a device called a *pinky pump*. Frozen-thawed pinkies and a small quantity of water (instead of water, one breeder I consulted uses a commercially offered reptile appetite stimulant called Stimulap) are placed into the syringe-like pinky pump, which purees the mice as they are injected through a small tube inserted down the snake's throat. The tube should be lubricated with vegetable oil or water before being inserted into the throat. Whenever possible, let an experienced person demonstrate proper force-feeding techniques before attempting them yourself.

Regurgitation

Regurgitation in any snake should be taken very seriously, as it could be the first indication of a disease that may threaten your entire collection. It may also point to shortcomings in your husbandry techniques, or a problem with your food supply.

Temperature. The most common cause of regurgitation is keeping snakes under temperatures that are too cool for adequate digestion. Food that remains in the stomach too long can turn rancid, releasing toxins that can harm or even kill a snake. Refer to the section on cage temperatures (page 29) to determine whether this could be the case. If so, increase the cage temperature to recommended levels and try feeding again after two or three days.

Pinky pump, used to force-feed newborn mice to neonates.

Overfeeding. This is another possible cause of regurgitation. Feeding too often is not natural. Feeding too many rodents at one time could mean that all of the prey will not fit into the snake's stomach. Prey that is too big can turn rancid before digestion is completed.

Frozen prey. When frozen rodents are involved, several possibilities should be considered. Rodents that have been stored too long may be suffering from freezer burn. Discard any rodents that are discolored, or have obvious deformities or tumors. If your frozen rodents were shipped to you and arrived partially or completely thawed, or if multiple snakes are regurgitating rodents from a new shipment, the whole batch may need to be thrown out. Ask your supplier about refund policies, and also whether the rodents might have been exposed to any pesticides or other chemicals. Be sure, too, that frozen rodents are always completely thawed before being fed to your snakes.

Other ingested material. Food is not the only thing that goes into your snake's stomach. Sand or wood chips used as the cage substrate often adheres to food and is swallowed, occasionally becoming lodged in the digestive tract and causing a blockage. The water dish is another area that requires investigation. Regular water changes, including a new dish, should be made every three to five days. Also change the water whenever any foreign matter is seen or after the snake has been observed soaking.

Stress factors. Being handled too soon after feeding and other stress factors may play a part in regurgitation. Cagemates or the lack of a suitable hiding place are other possible sources of stress.

Unless you feel you know the cause of the problem, it is best to put the affected snake into quarantine. If the problem continues, take the snake and the regurgitated rodent (I know—Yuck!) to your veterinarian for a culture. Be ready to explain all pertinent details about your husbandry practices.

Breeding

Should You Breed Your Boas?

Breeding your boas can add an exciting element to your hobby. It can also increase your knowledge, and you might even pass some knowledge along to other herpetoculturists. Even if your attempts fail, it is just as important to know what does not work as to know what does. By breeding your boas, you will be contributing your snakes' genes to future generations. Your offspring, whether sold to help pay for your hobby or traded for other species you may be interested in working with, can help reduce the demand on wild populations.

Risks

Although usually outweighed by the benefits and gratification of bringing forth new life, there are some risks involved in breeding that need to be considered. Most breeders use a period of cooling, referred to as *brumation*, to trigger the breeding cycle. Because such cooling does not occur naturally in the tropics, the experimental temperatures used have varied widely from breeder to breeder. Unfortunately, the results have also varied widely, even where strategies were similar. Methods that result in success for one breeder's boas may mean failure, even illness or death, for another's. The bottom line is that some cooling is beneficial for successful breeding, but too much and your boas' health will be at risk. The optimum temperature varies by species, and probably by individual animal, and therefore no perfect "recipe" for success exists. Regardless of the low temperature you choose, feeding must be halted. This

combination can leave boas weakened and more susceptible to disease or the effects of preexisting parasitic conditions. Considering the risks involved, only healthy snakes with good body weight should be selected for breeding.

Live-bearers

All boas are *ovoviviparous*—they bear live young. This may at first seem to be a tremendous advantage for breeders when compared to egg-layers like pythons, whose eggs require very specific temperature and humidity parameters to properly hatch. All breeders of egg-layers at some time will watch helplessly as a clutch of healthy-looking eggs withers and dies, and wonder what they did wrong. In this respect, breeding boas may be easier for the breeder, but live birth comes with an additional price to the snake, which must retain the developing embryos inside her body for extra months. Because many snakes will not feed while gravid, the reproductive process can take a much heavier toll in energy and bodily reserves on live-bearers. In addition, with live young being born later in the year, there is much less time for the snake to feed and regain body weight before the next breeding cycle begins. In the wild, boas may only reproduce biannually. In captivity, annual breeding is possible provided that females are fed heavily after brumation and parturition.

Age

Age, body weight, physical condition, and overall health are all key components to successful breeding. It is possible, of course, to feed some

Juvenile common boa constrictor with its mother. All baby snakes can take care of themselves from the moment of birth.

boas huge amounts of food, resulting in rapid growth, and breeding them in their second winter. This is often attempted by new breeders who think they see easy money coming. More than likely, however, the results include smaller litters and neonates, increased stillborn or deformed neonates and infertile "slugs," and a shortened lifespan for the female.

Small boas like rosy and sand boas can be bred after their third winter. This may also be possible for other boas as well, provided that they are at or near their adult size, with good body weight—heavy, but not obese. Males typically mature faster than females. If you can be patient and wait an extra year to breed a female, she will likely reward you with larger, healthier litters thereafter.

There is little evidence that old age reduces a snake's ability to reproduce or affects the number of young produced. Considering the long lifespans of which they are capable, it would seem likely that the rigors of annual brumation and breeding would take a toll long before any such "menopause" could occur. Before retiring or selling

off a boa due to dwindling litter sizes, try giving her a year off.

What Is Brumation?

Unlike true hibernation, in which an animal's brain activity and bodily functions drop to near-zero, brumation is better described as a period of reduced activity, in which bodily functions are slowed, but the animal may still move about. Brumation is more common in animals living in areas where winter temperatures do not remain below freezing. In the wild, brumating snakes will occasionally come out of their hiding places to drink, or to sun themselves on warm days.

The end of winter brumation signals breeding time for many animals, including snakes. The cool temperatures of winter are not just a timing trigger for behavioral patterns in snakes, but also appear to be crucial for physiological changes such as egg follicle development in females and sperm production in males. Even for tropical snakes such as boa constrictors, which do not experience cold temperatures in the wild, a brumation period is helpful, if not indispensable, to achieve successful breeding in captivity.

Because the digestive process is slowed considerably by cool temperatures, food eaten at this time could turn rancid in the stomach or intestines, resulting in regurgitation, illness, or even death. Brumating snakes generally will not eat, and in captivity must not be offered food. Obviously, this means the snake will be drawing energy from stored fat reserves, but at a faster rate than a snake that is truly hibernating. During brumation, a snake's immune system will also be reduced. Internal bacteria and parasites normally kept in check with warm temperatures may have the opportunity to overwhelm their host. For these reasons, your boas should not be exposed to brumation unless they are in perfect health, have been well-fed prior to cooling, and have excellent body weight. Cages should be thoroughly cleaned, and clean drinking water should always be available.

Initiating Brumation

If your boas are of adequate age, size, weight, and health, preparation for brumation can begin. Feeding should be increased during the months of August through October, more so for females than for males, and especially for females having produced offspring during the summer. Just remember that the goal is a snake that is heavy but not obese. Fat snakes often have little interest in breeding. Feeding should be stopped in late October or early November, and the snakes given two weeks to completely digest and pass their last meal from the digestive tract. If defecation does not occur, try handling the snake or soaking it in lukewarm water. During this time, if you utilize cage lighting, adjust your timers to begin reducing the hours of daylight. Photoperiod is usually considered less important to inducing breeding than temperature, and in fact, some breeders consider it of no importance. I personally prefer to imitate nature as much as possible, and therefore reduce not only the hours but also the intensity of the light, to match the natural reduction of winter sunlight. My rosy boas are brumated with my colubrids in a cool garage without any light at all, as this species would remain underground at similar temperatures in the wild.

Temperatures

Once all products of digestion have been eliminated, cooling can begin. Captive brumation for many snakes from North America and other temperate zones involves reducing the temperature into the mid to upper-50s F (13–15°C) and maintaining it at that level for approximately three months. The snakes are typically warmed back up in March, and breeding soon follows. While this works well for rosy boas, exposing boa constrictors and other tropical boas to prolonged periods of constantly cool temperatures can result in severe and possibly fatal respiratory illness, and increased risk of other diseases. Therefore, a modified brumation is utilized for tropical boas, using only moderately cool nights, but warm days. By slowly dropping the nighttime low temperature to approximately 70°F (21°C), and keeping or increasing the daytime high to 85–90°F (29–32°C), breeding can be induced while still maintaining a high level of resistance to disease. With the associated change in lighting, by the end of November, your tropical boas should be having long, cool nights, and short, warm days.

Your heating and cooling needs will be determined by where you live and the location of your cages. Unless you are brumating your entire collection, your breeders will have to be moved into a separate room. Achieving the correct daily cycle of temperatures requires some trial and error, so start early, long before any snakes are moved in. At night, cooling can be accomplished by cracking open a window or using an air conditioner. The first option is not very accurate, unless a thermostat-equipped heater is also employed to keep temperatures from falling too far. During the day, cages can be warmed individually, or you can warm the entire room using an electric space heater, but be careful to exercise every precaution with space heaters to avoid fire hazards. Even if the heater has adjustable heat settings, it is a wise safety precaution to plug it into a thermostat that is set a couple of degrees warmer. If the heater ever fails to shut off, the thermostat will act as a safety backup and shut it off. Entire collections have been lost to malfunctioning or forgotten space heaters. Attach any air conditioner and heaters to timers for consistent, hands-off operation.

Digital thermometers with a memory feature for maximum and minimum temperatures can be found at most hardware and consumer electronics stores. Some have a remote sensor and two displays for indoor and outdoor readings, perfect for monitoring both room and internal cage temperatures. Record temperatures and reset the memory on a daily basis. It's a good idea to have multiple thermometers in order to verify results and catch malfunctioning units.

Introduction and Mating

In mid- to late December, it is time to begin putting your males and females together. One male can be used to breed two or even more females. Multiple males are considered important by many to elicit breeding, but of course the exact parentage of resulting offspring will be uncertain if the group is not observed. The enclosure used for breeding trials with multiple males should be sufficiently large, with multiple hide boxes, so that submissive males can separate themselves from dominant males.

It is possible to maintain a breeding

One of the male's two hemipenes is everted during copulation. Physical differences in hemipenis structure between species is one reason why cross-breeding snakes is rarely possible.

pair or group together throughout the entire cooling period; however, a better breeding response is achieved when the snakes are kept apart and then introduced at the appropriate time. This also reduces stress on the snakes, and because newly-introduced snakes will often initiate courtship right away, the success of a pairing is less likely to be in question. Pairs or groups can be left together for days, or even weeks, occasionally separating and reintroducing the snakes if breeding activity is not observed. If there seems to be no interest after repeated reintroductions, the disinterested parties can be replaced with more willing partners.

The Mating Act

Most breeders prefer to introduce the females into the male's cage. If the male is interested, he will immediately begin chasing the female, usually in quick, jerky movements, flicking out his tongue and rubbing his chin along her back. The male's spurs, located on either side of the cloaca, are sometimes brought into play to stimulate the female. A receptive female, typically moving slowly or with the same jerky movements as the male, will allow the male to rub his chin on her back as he aligns his body along hers, and may even lift her tail. When the tails are aligned, the male wraps his tail underneath the female, and inserts one hemipenis into her cloaca. Mating can last from a few minutes to a few hours. Occasionally, a female will lose interest before the male does, and may attempt to crawl away, dragging the male with her. Multiple successful copulations are recommended to ensure fertilization.

Most boa constrictors and other tropical boas will breed during the cooling period in December or January, and sometimes in February or beyond. Brumation should be terminated by gradually increasing cage temperatures to their normal levels beginning in late January. Resume feeding if the snakes will eat. If the female does not show signs of being gravid, breeding trials should be continued through March. Argentine boa constrictors, coming as they do from more southern and cooler regions, can be cycled at a slightly cooler range of 60–65°F (16–18°C) for the nighttime low and 80–85°F (27–29°C) for the daytime high. Copulation in Argentine boas typically occurs after the end of cooling.

For rosy boas and other temperate-zone boas brumated at constant and much cooler temperatures, breeding also occurs after the arrival of spring. Terminate brumation at the end of February by slowly raising the temperature and hours of daylight over a period of several days back to the normal summertime schedule. After a few more days of warm temperatures, offer a small meal. Unless the meal is refused or regurgitated, resume normal feeding for the male and heavy feeding for the female. Begin placing the female with the male in late April. Rosy boas typically breed from late April through June. Continue separating and reintroducing the pair until several matings have taken place or the female appears to be gravid.

Tips to Induce Breeding

A nonreceptive female will flee from the advances of the male, indicating that she is not yet ready to breed. If it is the male who is not interested, or if breeding attempts continuously get no results, there are several things you may do to help. Introducing a male immediately after the female sheds her skin often gets good results. Don't even take the shed skin out of the cage.

Male combat may stimulate both sexes. Combat is often no more than a wrestling match to establish dominance and breeding rights, and typi-

Combat between males for dominance. Combat can stimulate males and even females into breeding. Males should be observed closely, and separated if biting occurs.

cally no blood is drawn, but biting may result in severe injuries. Be prepared to remove the extra male immediately if biting is observed, if it is excessively fearful of the dominant male, or if the males constantly combat each other while ignoring the females completely. Even sexually immature males can be used in this role. The shed skin of another male may also be effective.

Other tricks to induce breeding include lightly misting the snakes with water and moving them into a new and unfamiliar enclosure. Passing storm fronts and low-pressure weather systems have also been credited with increased breeding activity. It is even suggested that placing the snakes together in a cloth bag and giving them a bumpy ride in your car might help.

Indications of Fertility

Some breeders will take the opportunity immediately after mating to check on the fertility of the male. By inserting a swab into the female's cloaca, a semen sample can be obtained and transferred to a slide for observation under a microscope.

The earliest and best indication of fertility in the female is a mid-body swelling as the mature ova are

Female Brazilian rainbow boa with neonates and unfertilized slugs. Note wire mesh, offering neonates refuge from being crushed by the female.

even more critical. A female faced with only two choices—too cold or too hot—will often choose too hot. Aberrant appearances caused by poor gestation temperatures are defects, not inheritable traits, so don't maintain gravid females under suboptimum conditions in the hope of creating marketable mutations.

Most females will spend all of their time curled up in the basking area. A peculiar behavior of gravid females is lying on their sides, sometimes to the point of being nearly upside-down. Whether this is an effort to expose the developing embryos to greater warmth, or just more comfortable, is known only to the mother-to-be. Females may be a bit testy at this time, and should not be held or moved if it can be avoided.

Although gravid females will often refuse food, small food items should be offered occasionally and may be accepted. The idea is to provide some extra vitamins and minerals and reduce the depletion of the female's reserves. Feeding too often or feeding prey that is too large can cause problems, as the developing embryos take up considerable space in the snake's narrow body. Whether the snake eats or not, clean water should always be available close by.

The gestation period for boas averages from four to eight months. As the due date approaches, the female may become restless and move away from the basking area to a cooler spot. At this point, there is not much more to do but watch and wait, and begin planning on how you will house and feed the neonates when they arrive.

released from the ovaries. This swelling may only be apparent for a very short time, so it is important to examine females on a daily basis. Ova may be released before copulation and await fertilization in the oviduct, or even weeks after copulation and be fertilized by retained sperm. Placing the female with the male at this time, particularly if copulation has not yet been observed, may increase your chances of successful breeding.

Care of Gravid Females

A gravid female will appear quite large in girth in the posterior two-thirds of her body and will usually cease feeding. A warm basking area, up to 95°F (35°C), should be provided, either using a basking light or heating pad. Failure to provide adequate heat does not always prolong the gestation period, but may result in aberrant colors or patterns and serious health and development problems for the offspring. Excessive temperatures can also be extremely detrimental, perhaps more so than inadequate temperatures, making a temperature gradient

When the Offspring Arrive

After parturition (birth), neonates are enclosed in a thin, clear membrane, from which they will break out almost immediately. The membrane is attached to the snake at the stomach, and this attachment should also be broken easily. In most cases, your role in the delivery will be limited. You'll simply look in the cage and find a batch of healthy neonates already out and exploring their world. The young are born with all the equipment and instincts they need to survive. Remember that when you reach in to pick them up!

It is rare for a boa to eat her young, although unfertilized ova are frequently consumed. With the large size of some boas, however, the chance does exist for neonates to be crushed in the confined space of a cage or hide box. For this reason, as well as for easier observation and accurate record keeping, each neonate should be moved into its own cage or plastic shoebox as soon as possible. Pine shavings or newspaper make good substrate to hide under. Cardboard tubes from paper towel rolls make good, disposable hiding places.

Neonates should be observed for signs of dehydration prior to their first shedding. For neonate rainbow boas, or for any neonates that seem dehydrated, use slightly dampened paper towels and lightly mist the enclosure as needed. I have found that paper towels are much less likely than newspaper to get moldy when damp.

Neonates will shed their first skin several days after birth. At that time, you can offer a first meal of a pinkie or fuzzy mouse or rat. Try frozen-thawed first, and get your neonates started right. If they continually refuse, try leaving a live one in the cage overnight (remember, we're talking harmless baby rodents without teeth here). Neonates have adequate stored energy from their absorbed yolks so you should not be in a big hurry to resort to force-feeding. Refer to pages 40–41, Convincing a Difficult Feeder, and only resort to force-feeding after two to three months for large species,

Many boa constrictors, such as this Brazilian red-tail, often begin life as gray juveniles, changing to brown, pink and red as they mature.

and one to two months for small ones. Some rosy boas will not eat until their first spring—breeders may brumate non-feeders for a short period after birth.

After giving birth, the female will be tired and weak. Let her rest, and offer her small meals to begin with, especially if she has not eaten for several months. If she has lost a lot of weight, or if it is very late in the year, it might be best not to try breeding her again during the next breeding season. If you do decide to breed her, you will have to start feeding heavily soon.

Unexpected Problems

If you are fortunate to be able to witness the birth process, watch for any neonate that may have difficulty breaking free of its membrane. When there is a dry substrate like newspaper, it is possible for the membrane to stick and dry out quickly, possibly entangling the snake. A pair of scissors can be used to open the membrane if needed, or to cut the umbilicus about an inch (25 mm) from the stomach if it will not break off on its own. Some blood vessels are present in the membrane, so be prepared for the sight of blood.

Unlike mammals, in ovoviviparous snakes the embryos do not develop attached to, and drawing nutrients from, the mother. Instead, the process could better be described as unshelled eggs being incubated inside the female. Each egg is produced surrounded by only a shell membrane, with a large amount of yolk from which the growing embryo will derive its nutrients. As the embryo grows, the yolk shrinks, until it is finally absorbed into the neonate's body cavity. This explains why gravid snakes start off large and stay that way, instead of growing steadily throughout gestation. Occasionally, a neonate will be born with the yolk not yet fully absorbed. If this happens, place the snake in a small tank or plastic shoebox with damp paper towels as a substrate, giving the snake time to absorb the remaining yolk. Placing a small hide box over the snake will help discourage it from moving around.

If any neonates are born with serious deformities, euthanasia may be required. I prefer to place the snake in a zip-loc bag and put it in the freezer. It's sad to look at the snake and know what could have been, but it has to be done. Multiple deformities and color aberrations within a litter may indicate that gestation temperatures were consistently too low or too high.

It is not uncommon for live-bearing snakes to pass unfertilized ova, sometimes referred to as "slugs," along with live neonates. Large numbers of slugs may indicate shortcomings in the female's preparedness for breeding (i.e., too young, insufficient weight), in the male's fertility, or in the number of successful copulations. Review your methods and see if improvements can be made in the next breeding season.

Occasionally, a female may be unable to deliver unfertilized ova or dead neonates. If your boa has detectable lumps after parturition, consult with your veterinarian for advice and possibly X-rays. In worst-case scenarios, surgery may be required to remove the object. Failure to do so could result in permanent sterility or death for the snake.

Record Keeping

There are so many details involved in the breeding process that you will never remember them all by next breeding season—but whether your female has a huge, healthy litter or none at all, you'll want to understand why. By keeping careful daily records of your methods, photoperiod, temperatures, pairings, observed or suspected copulations, female gestation behavior and use of basking sites, you will have everything you need to repeat your success or help avoid another disappointment next year. You can also discuss your notes with successful breeders to see where improvements might be made. Remember, those who don't learn from their mistakes are doomed to repeat them.

Genetics: Breeding a Better Boa

For breeders with a preference for colors as nature intended, the ultimate goal is to produce offspring with exceptional color and sharp, clear patterns. Through careful selection of breeding stock, aggressive culling of undesirable animals, and by pairing only the finest animals together, breeders can offer extremely attractive snakes that command higher prices. In recent years, however, the popularity and availability of snakes with unusual genetic color and pattern mutations have increased dramatically. Perhaps this fascination arises out of our need for something new and exciting. As our world quickly runs out of new species to discover, we turn instead to new variations of old favorites. Although not yet as common in boas as in rat snakes or kingsnakes, additional "strains" or "phases" of various boas are certain to be discovered in the future. Initial offerings of new strains often come with a hefty price tag. Juvenile albino boa constrictors, for instance, first appeared on the market for around $10,000 each. Obviously, such financially rewarding snakes are in extremely high demand by breeders. But where do these snakes originally come from, and how can desirable traits be continued or even improved?

Traits and Genes

Physical traits are determined by the genetic code contained within every cell nucleus, on structures called *chromosomes*. Chromosomes, which are actually individual DNA molecules, always exist as pairs. The total number of pairs varies in different types of animals. Offspring receive one chromosome of each pair from the mother, while the other is received from the father. On each chromosome, there exists a specific region, called a gene, that controls each physical trait, such as eye color in humans, or skin color in snakes. Each *gene* is located at a precise location on the chromosome. The gene for a specific trait is located at the same site on each chromosome of a pair, and it is these paired genes that ultimately determine the trait. To add to the complexity, many traits are influenced by more than one gene pair.

An animal's overall physical appearance, referred to as its *phenotype*, is determined by the sum total of all of its genes, or *genotype*. The terms pheno-type and genotype may also be applied in a stricter sense to a specific trait, such as skin color or pattern, and the gene or genes that control that trait. Some of the common skin color phenotypes seen in snakes are albino, leucistic (white), piebald (areas of white and normal color/pattern), xan-thic (yellow), amelanistic (without black) or anerythristic (without red). In the wild, unusual phenotypes may be the result of a natural mutation within a gene. Whether the mutation gets passed along or not depends largely on whether the phenotype enhances the animal's ability to survive.

Let us return to a single pair of genes that control a specific trait. Sometimes the genes are for the same phenotype. Both genes may agree, for example, on what the skin color will be. In this case, the animal is said to be *homozygous* for that particular trait. When the two genes are for different phenotypes, however, one gene often dominates the other and determines the outcome. Such animals are said to be *heterozygous*, because they carry a *dominant* gene for one phe-notype and a *recessive* gene for another. Recessive traits, such as albinism, can only be expressed when a recessive gene is paired with a similar recessive gene. The table below shows the results of the three possible combi-nations of normal and albino genes. Dominant genes are always shown using capital letters, recessive genes using lowercase. For all of our exam-ples, we will use 'N' for the gene for nor-mal color and 'a' for the albino gene.

Maternal Gene	Paternal Gene	Result
N	N	Normal coloration, homozygous for normal color
N	a	Normal coloration, heterozygous for albinism
a	a	Albino, homozygous for albinism

N = dominant gene for normal color, a = recessive gene for albinism

Inheriting Traits

So, how do genes get passed from parents to offspring? During a process called *meiosis*, single cells divide to produce two *gametes* (egg or sperm cells). Each gamete receives one half of each chromosome pair, and therefore one half of each gene pair. During fertilization, a male and female gamete unite to form a *zygote*. Each chromosome finds and pairs up with its matching chromosome from the other gamete. The genes, once again paired, immediately begin influencing the developing embryo.

For any given trait, such as skin color, unless both parents are homozygous for the same phenotype, the phenotype of future offspring becomes a game of chance. However, by knowing the genotype of prospective parents, and understanding which genes are dominant and which are recessive, knowledgeable breeders can use tables called *Punnett squares* to forecast the outcome. In a Punnett square, the genes of one parent are assigned to the columns of the table, and the genes of the other parent are assigned to the rows. Remember that paired genes are split apart during meiosis, with either gene of one parent being capable of being paired to either gene of the other during fertilization. In a Punnett square, the intersections of columns and rows show each possible pairing, and also the statistical probability of each. Let's look at a Punnett square for two boas that are homozygous for normal color.

	N	N
N	NN	NN
N	NN	NN

Parents: Both homozygous for normal color (NN)
Offspring probabilities: 100 percent homozygous for normal color (NN)

That was easy. Because each parent can only pass along gametes with the gene for normal color, the fertilized zygote can only have paired genes for normal color. But what if one of the parents was heterozygous for albinism? The Punnett square below shows this.

	N	a
N	NN	Na
N	NN	Na

Parents: One homozygous for normal color (NN), one heterozygous for albinism (Na)
Offspring probabilities: 50 percent homozygous for normal color (NN), 50 percent heterozygous for albinism (Na)

Strategies for Breeding Albino Boas

Without its camouflage coloration, an albino snake is not only easily spotted by predators, but also by its prey, and therefore rarely survives in the wild long enough to reproduce. Occasionally, one is discovered and finds its way into the pet trade, where, if no other albinos exist for the species, a breeder might shell out tens of thousands of dollars to procure it. In other cases, lucky breeders find one or more albinos mixed in with a litter of neonates from a pair of normally colored adults, indicating that both parents are heterozygous for albinism. Normally colored neonates in the same litter may be homozygous for normal coloration or heterozygous for albinism, as shown below.

	N	a
N	NN	Na
a	Na	aa

Parents: Both heterozygous for albinism (Na)
Offspring probabilities: 25 percent homozygous for normal color (NN), 50 percent heterozygous for albinism (Na), 25 percent albino (aa)

Many breeders sell normally colored offspring from heterozygous parents labeled as "possibly heterozygous for albinism," at a slightly higher than normal price. The only way to tell is to raise and breed them to an albino or a known heterozygous mate, with at least one albino offspring resulting. If possible, breed known and suspected heterozygous animals to albinos, as shown below, to help avoid getting additional "unknowns."

	a	**a**
N	Na	Na
a	aa	aa

Parents: One heterozygous for albinism (Na), one albino (aa)
Offspring probabilities: 50 percent heterozygous for albinism(Na), 50 percent albino (aa)

Once albinos have been acquired, confirming the presence of the recessive gene, selective breeding can be used to produce more. The only way to guarantee that a litter of neonates will be 100 percent albino is to breed two albinos to each other. If you're the lucky breeder who just had multiple albinos appear in a litter, you can do this, but you will also be inbreeding siblings. Inbreeding can bring out additional and often undesirable recessive traits and genetic defects, especially as inbreeding is continued on successive generations.

The resolution to the problem of inbreeding is referred to as *outcrossing*, breeding the albinos to unrelated, normally colored animals (assuming no unrelated albinos are available) to introduce new genes, then breeding their subsequent offspring back together. Albino or heterozygous males can also be bred to a number of females, increasing the number of genetic lines. Obviously, outcrossing

Genetic mutations like this albino boa constrictor command high prices from collectors.

will take much more time to produce albino offspring for sale, but it will have to be practiced to some extent where the desired genes come from a single or very small number of founders. The alternative may be genetically defective snakes that nobody will want.

Always remember that Punnett squares show all *possible* pairings of genes after meiosis, but only *statistical* probabilities of phenotype ratios. With millions of sperms and possibly dozens of egg cells meeting at random, this does not preclude the possibility, especially in a small litter, of all offspring having the same phenotype. Genetics can be a bit confusing at first, but can also open up a world of opportunities for the dedicated breeder.

Parasites and Diseases

Prevention and Identification

The top three killers of reptiles in captivity are inadequate nutrition, diseases, and parasites. Due to their whole-animal diet and lack of a need for special lighting, nutritional problems are much less common in snakes than in other reptiles. The dangers of diseases and parasites, however, must be taken very seriously. It is too easy to avoid looking closely, to ignore or dismiss the signs, or to convince yourself that all is well, up until the day the animal dies. Your boa deserves better.

Prevention of diseases and parasitic outbreaks begins by selecting only healthy-looking snakes. Problems are not always immediately apparent, so strict adherence to quarantine procedures is crucial. Having a fecal exam performed by your veterinarian will take much of the worry and guesswork out of dealing with new arrivals, and save you a lot of heartache later on. Regularly cleaning and disinfecting cages, combined with quick removal of feces and shed skins, reduces your snake's exposure to potentially harmful bacteria and helps to control parasite loading. You may not be able to eliminate harmful bacteria and parasites completely, but make every effort to kill as many as you can. Snakes that eat well and are kept warm and free of undue stress will have a much better chance of coping with the rest.

The symptoms of diseases and parasites, especially internal parasites, are often similar. Basically, any unexplainable physical or behavioral manifestation should be a cause for concern. Symptoms to watch for include:

- refusal to feed
- regurgitation
- weight loss
- slow growth
- dehydration
- constipation
- runny, discolored, foul-smelling, or bloody stools
- lesions of the skin or mouth
- blisters or cysts
- swelling
- sneezing or wheezing
- inability or reluctance to close mouth
- lethargy
- neurological difficulties

If a problem is suspected, don't wait for the situation to get so bad as to be incurable. Snakes may give only subtle clues when something is wrong, and sometimes none at all. Conditions are often well advanced before being noticeable. Place the animal in isolation and begin treatment immediately, or take the animal to a qualified veterinarian. Not all veterinarians are experienced in treating reptiles. I highly recommend finding one who is, and long before his or her services are required.

Important knowledge can be gained even after death. It may seem unreasonable to spend money on a dead snake, but a necropsy (animal autopsy) can identify pathogens or lapses in husbandry that can improve the health and future care of your collection. Don't deny your mistakes—correct them! Deceased specimens should be refrigerated, not frozen, and delivered to your veterinarian as soon as possible.

Treatment

Treating reptile diseases is a fairly recent and developing specialty within veterinary medicine, a field previously dedicated to the health of dogs, cats, and livestock. But before veterinarians began seeing enough cold-blooded patients to take much interest, dedicated herpetoculturists were already searching for cures for their reptiles' ills. Due to financial considerations, and perhaps the fact that reptile owners are often (but not always!) less emotionally attached to their pets than dog or cat owners, many herpetoculturists continue to treat their animals themselves. If you wish to pursue this area, entire volumes have recently been published on the subject (see Useful Literature and Addresses, page 89). If not, sound husbandry practices and a veterinarian qualified and experienced in diagnosing and treating reptiles will serve you well.

The following sections are intended to familiarize you with some of the diseases that could affect your boa, emphasizing just how devastating those diseases can be, and how the efforts required to cure them far outweigh those needed to prevent them. Although some drug and dosage information is provided, it is not my intention to provide a step-by-step guide for treatment. I leave that to the experts, for the simple reason that not even the experts always agree. By reviewing the available literature and consulting with reptile veterinarians, I have determined that the drugs, dosages, and procedures that follow are generally accepted as being effective. In an area where recommendations are constantly changing, it would be inappropriate to state that they will be 100 percent effective, or that they represent the only course of action available. They are also not intended to be used for treating other types of reptiles, or even other snakes besides boas.

Advancements in drugs and methods are sure to continue at a rapid pace, for the benefit of all. Keepers who take the responsibility for their boa's health seriously should make the attempt to stay abreast of the latest research and drug recommendations. And even if you plan to treat your snake yourself, get to know your veterinarian. You may still need cultures, fecal analysis, or X-rays—and antibiotics and hypodermic syringes are not sold to just anyone.

Regardless of the disease being treated, maintaining a diurnal temperature at the high end of the snake's preferred range, with a slight drop of only a few degrees at night, can greatly improve the patient's chances of recovering. If the snake will eat, normal feeding should be continued.

The Danger of Parasite Loading

Many of the parasites that can harm your snake in large numbers are quite common in small numbers. Wild-caught specimens are often afflicted, yet seem perfectly healthy. So why should we worry? Because in the wild, internal and external parasite loads are naturally kept low through the processes of shedding and defecation, and the snake's habit of constantly moving on. External parasites leaving the host to lay their eggs are left behind to search for a new host. At the same time, thermoregulation allows the snake to always choose the best temperature for its defenses. Now consider your boa in captivity, where there is no escaping from feces or shed skins except through your intervention. The longer the snake is exposed, the better the chances for adult and larval parasites to reinfest the host. External parasites still leave the host to lay their eggs, but not only do they return to reinfest the host, so do their thousands of offspring. The parasite loading continues to explode until the host's resistance completely fails.

External Parasites

The two external parasites most commonly encountered on snakes are **mites** and **ticks**. Both are bloodsuckers, and as such can cause dehydration, anemia, and even death when present in large numbers. They can also be the cause of poor shedding and skin infections, and can act as vectors for spreading disease through your collection. Even in small numbers, they can be annoying to the host. An infested snake may spend hours or days curled up in the water dish, or cruise its enclosure endlessly, sometimes rubbing its head on walls and cage furniture. The result is a weakened, stressed snake that is now at risk for skin sores, as well as various infections from rubbing its mouth, nose, and eyes against possibly bacteria-laden objects.

Mites are typically acquired from new arrivals and other collections. Ticks are most often found on wild-caught specimens. Both should be dealt with quickly and completely.

Mites

They may not be the most dangerous parasite that can infest a reptile collection, but few keepers who have dealt with them would disagree that mites are certainly the most irritating. Mites can be difficult to spot, and even more difficult to eradicate once entrenched in a large collection. Your best offense is a good defense—never let them get into your collection to begin with! Mites most often arrive on newly purchased animals. Handling other people's snakes, or letting other keepers handle yours, is another way to pick them up, as is buying used cages or accessories and not properly cleaning and disinfecting them.

To identify mites, look closely around the eyes and in the fold of skin under a snake's chin. Mites are very tiny, and brown to black in color. They are more easily spotted when engorged with blood, at which time they may be nearly as big as the head of a pin. They are easily spotted on light-colored snakes such as an emerald tree boa or albino boa constrictor, but blend in well with the black markings and speckling of a common boa constrictor. The fine white droppings mites leave behind can be a telltale sign on a dark snake. By holding these snakes up against a light background, you can search along the silhouette of the back for tiny, moving bumps. Wiping the snake with a white handkerchief, or soaking the snake in tepid (room temperature) water for 10 to 15 minutes should dislodge at least a few mites if they are present. A good magnifier is helpful in determining if a spot is a mite or just a speck of dirt. Dirt doesn't have legs.

Simple, vigilant quarantine procedures will help you stop mites early. A close inspection should be made when the snake is purchased, and treatment started immediately if mites are detected. Even if none are found, keep checking and rechecking throughout the quarantine period. Two mites will quickly become two thousand.

Mites are extremely mobile, and leave the host in order to lay their eggs in corners, cracks, and crevices. If you discover that your snake has mites, assume they've spread to the cage and beyond, and immediately declare war. Simplify everything by having only a hide box, water dish, and newspaper in the cage. Any rocks or branches should be thoroughly cleaned and disinfected and put aside until all mites are completely eradicated. If small aquariums or plastic sweater boxes are used, swap the snake into a new one every day, with new paper, water dish, and hide box. Whether you decide to use an insecticide to kill the adult mites or not, the life cycle must be broken by destroying the eggs, which can hatch out within 30 hours of being laid. If the cage cannot be replaced daily, it must be washed and disinfected daily and the substrate replaced. Imagine that every crack and crevice contains mites and mite eggs.

Treatments to kill mites include the use of No-Pest Strips, Trichlorfon (Neguvon), and Sevin Dust. Soaking the snake can also kill a lot of mites, but some will survive on the head and in air pockets under the scales. A 1-inch (25 mm) piece of No Pest Strip, placed in an empty film canister with air holes punched out to avoid direct contact, can be placed inside or on top of the cage. Note of caution: Prolonged exposure to No-Pest Strips has been reported to cause temporary nervous disorders in snakes. Opinions on the proper length of exposure vary from two to three hours to two to three days, but certainly such strips should not be used constantly. I have never experienced any problems, nor much notable success, using No-Pest Strips, but continue to use them as an added safety measure against stragglers after other treatments are complete. Trichlorfon, diluted to 0.16 percent (1/50 of normal product strength of 8 percent) solution, has been proven effective when sprayed on the snake and enclosure, allowed to air dry and left for 24 hours. Sevin Dust can be liberally applied to the snake and its enclosure for three to four hours at a time. Always remove the water dish during any insecticide treatment.

My preferred and proven method of treating mites is to use Mycodex flea and tick spray. The 0.2 percent pyrethrins spray is diluted with three parts water (to 0.05 percent), sprayed on a paper towel and wiped lightly onto the snake. The original cage is sprayed heavily, especially joints and corners, and after sitting for several minutes the excess is spread around and wiped out with a paper towel, leaving a thin film to air dry. The outside of the cage and the shelves or rack on which it rests are also wiped with the spray, to help kill any egg-layers coming or going. If the snake must be placed back inside, the cage is first allowed to dry and air out for at least an hour. This process is repeated for two more days.

I prefer to transfer infested snakes to plastic sweater boxes in a separate room for a complete change of sweater box and accessories every day. I sometimes use the pyrethrin spray to treat the boxes before moving the snake in, but have generally found that wiping the snake down daily for two to three days, combined with daily box exchanges, quickly eradicates the mites. I then continue the daily box exchanges and inspections until I'm 100 percent convinced they're gone. The snake will also not be put back into its cage until that, too, is free of mites. If all snakes have been removed from the room where mites were found, I will even spray the carpet and behind shelves with common household bug spray, but I never use this type of bug spray inside or too close to my cages. Mites can survive weeks without a blood meal, so don't relax too soon.

Ticks

Although much larger than mites, ticks are still often difficult to spot. Their dark, flat, rounded bodies can closely resemble the scales under which they burrow. When engorged with blood, however, their size usually gives them away. Ticks are well-known carriers of disease, for snakes and humans. Snakes from a pet shop, especially known imports, should be checked closely. As with mites, ticks

Ticks are sometimes found on newly imported snakes.

prefer protected areas such as around the eyes and the cloaca.

Once spotted, ticks should be pulled out with forceps or tweezers. Use firm, steady pressure instead of a sudden pull, so that the head is pulled out. A small amount of flesh, softened by the tick's secretions, may be pulled out as well, but this is fine. Treat the wound with hydrogen peroxide or Betadine (povidone iodine), and finish up with Neosporin antiseptic ointment.

Internal Parasites

Internal parasites can cause several different types of harm. At the very least, parasites living in the intestinal tract steal nutrients from the host. Heavy infestations can result in a healthy-looking boa that either loses weight or fails to grow, despite being an excellent feeder. Other parasites are not so subtle, sucking blood, boring through tissue and organs, blocking passageways, and spreading bacteria. In many cases, the existence of these parasites is not detected until necropsy.

Some breeders and importers dealing with large numbers of animals choose to treat all imports and new arrivals, using a range of drugs known to be effective against the most common parasites. If you have only one or

a small number of snakes, a fecal examination by your veterinarian will give a much more accurate indication of just what treatment, if any, is required.

Nematodes

Nematodes comprise a large group of worms, including roundworms, hookworms, and lungworms, most often found in the digestive tract but occasionally present in the lungs or airways. Roundworms present in large numbers within the intestine can steal much of the nutrients from the host, resulting in weight loss, malnutrition, or failure to grow adequately. Hookworms draw blood through the intestinal wall, causing inflammation, anemia, and peritonitis. Heavy infestations of lungworms can lead to pneumonia. Nematode larvae migrating through tissues and organs can cause direct damage or obstructions. Although spaghetti-like adult roundworms may occasionally be seen with the naked eye in stools or regurgitated food, detection of nematodes is typically made using microscopic fecal analysis.

Treatment. Panacur (fenbendazole), administered orally at a dose of 100mg/kg, is effective and extremely safe for treating nematodes. Repeat treatment every two weeks for a total of three doses. The ability of some nematodes to gain access to the host directly through the skin makes strict cage cleaning and immediate removal of feces imperative. Cleaning and disinfecting of water dishes, as well as close attention to personal hygiene, will help prevent the spread of nematodes to previously unaffected animals.

Tapeworms (Cestodes) and Flukes (Trematodes)

Although unrelated, tapeworms and flukes are similar in their life cycles and effective treatment. As adults, both can be seen with the naked eye—tapeworms as long, flat worms in the cloaca or feces, and flukes as short, dark worms in the mouth, esophagus, cloaca, or feces. Any parasites observed on the host can be gently removed with tweezers or a cotton swab. Kidney damage is also possible from renal flukes. Both groups have an indirect life cycle, requiring an intermediate invertebrate or mammalian host in which the larvae can develop. It is through the ingestion of the intermediate hosts that snakes acquire these parasites. The absence of intermediate hosts in captivity effectively prevents their spread through a collection. By using frozen food animals, further introduction is also unlikely. Despite their self-limiting nature, however, tapeworms and flukes are capable of causing internal damage and should be eliminated.

Treatment. Droncit (praziquantel), administered subcutaneously or orally at a dose of 5–8mg/kg, is effective.

Protozoa

Protozoan parasites are naturally occurring and quite common in all reptiles. In the wild, most cause few problems, but under stressful or sub-optimum conditions of captivity, the potential exists for these microorganisms to multiply to problematic levels. Diarrhea or foul-smelling stools, and stools containing noticeable blood, bile or mucous, are typical indications. A fecal exam on a fresh stool can be used to identify the specific organism involved. If left untreated, some types, such as *Entamoeba invadens*, can spread to other organs and tissues via the circulatory system.

Treatment. The treatment of choice for boas is Flagyl (metronidazole), administered orally at a dose of 50–100mg/kg. Some literature suggests higher doses, but others consider that risky. Repeat after one week if needed. Flagyl should not be used on gravid snakes.

Another serious protozoan threat is the coccidian parasite *Cryptosporidium*, which has been responsible for some devastating epidemics in snake collections. As with many other internal parasites, these microorganisms can be spread through contaminated food and water, as well as improper hygiene. Lesions in the stomach caused by this parasite result in regurgitation of food. Swelling and thickening of the stomach wall follows, which can sometimes be felt externally or even seen. Cryptosporidiosis is an extremely contagious disease, for which early medical diagnosis is difficult and no cure exists. Any case of regurgitation for which no obvious explanation can be found, or where subsequent meals are also regurgitated, should be taken seriously. Isolation and diligent hygiene are a must. Euthanasia is often suggested for confirmed cases.

Diseases

Snakes are susceptible to a number of diseases, both viral and bacterial. While viruses have the potential to virtually wipe out an entire collection in a short period of time, it is bacterial infections that claim the most victims overall. Unlike the Gram-positive bacteria common to humans, the pathogenic organisms typically found in reptiles and implicated in many diseases and deaths are the Gram-negative bacteria, mostly *Pseudomonas*. Ross and Marzec, in *The Bacterial Diseases of Reptiles* (Institute for Herpetological Research, Santa Barbara, CA, 1984) report finding a 100 percent incidence of *Pseudomonas* in several boid collections examined, as well as in the water dishes of importers' holding facilities. Nearly every snake processed through the pet trade can be expected to harbor *Pseudomonas*, and possibly other Gram-negative bacteria, by the time it

Star-gazing disease, or just looking? Watch for continuing behavior and additional symptoms.

arrives in your collection. Because bacteria can be passed from snake to snake, and from female directly to offspring, even purchasing a captive-bred juvenile directly from the source will not guarantee a pathogen-free snake. Only your veterinarian can tell you if your snake is pathogen-free, but unless you've just purchased an extremely valuable animal and are prepared to isolate it from other affected reptiles, save your money. Bacteria can be suppressed, but never eliminated completely.

Bacteria are opportunistic, often benign in low concentrations but always waiting for an injury, stress, or weakness in the host to gain the upper hand. Providing your boa with the recommended warmth, while keeping it free of parasites and undue stress, will allow it to mount the necessary defenses to keep bacteria in check. Cages should not only be cleaned, but disinfected as well. Cleaning solutions are not always antibacterial, and disinfectants are not always good cleaning agents.

Some bacteria occasionally found in snakes can be transmitted to people, perhaps the best known being

Salmonella. Although rarely dangerous to healthy adults, there is an increased risk to very young children and those with compromised immune systems. Precautions include washing hands after handling snakes or cleaning cages, avoiding washing equipment and water dishes with the family's supper dishes, using antibacterial soaps and detergents, and limiting exposure of young children to animals and freshly shed skins.

Star Gazer's Disease

Star gazing, pointing the nose straight up into the air, can be a symptom of a number of possible diseases and conditions. First of all, do not panic if your boa is suddenly observed in this position. It may just be looking around, and freezing in any one position for several minutes is not uncommon. If the behavior continues, however, or is associated with other suspicious symptoms, consult your veterinarian immediately for a diagnosis. Some causes may be treatable if caught early. For example, a nose-up posture is often associated with respiratory infections and other afflictions where mucous buildup makes breathing difficult. Wheezing or nasal discharge helps identify such cases.

While star gazing may result from almost any disease of the nervous system, the term "star gazer's disease," in its most commonly accepted and dangerous form, refers to a retroviral neurological disease known as *inclusion body disease.* The disease typically begins with regurgitation, progressing into head tremors, star gazing, disorientation, or paralysis. The disease is highly contagious and untreatable, and the final outcome is death. Strict quarantine or euthanasia is a must. Boas have been implicated as carriers of this disease, capable of spreading it to other species even when the host appears unaffected.

Mouth Rot

Necrotizing or ulcerative stomatitis, commonly known as mouth rot, affects the gums and mucous membranes of the mouth. It is a serious, progressive disease that, if not treated quickly and aggressively, will spread into other tissues and bones of the head resulting in death. Swelling and discoloration of the gums, in conjunction with an unwillingness or inability to close the mouth, are typical symptoms. Injuries to the mouth, such as rodent bites, abrasions from constantly rubbing the nose against screening or rough objects, and bruises from striking against glass can all lead to an increased risk of disease, especially when combined with a dirty cage or suboptimum temperatures. Remember that any snake cruising a cage containing fecal matter will invariably spread minute amounts of feces wherever it crawls, including glass doors or walls, where bacteria will continue to multiply. Glass is foreign to snakes, and they spend a great deal of time pushing their heads against it. Herpetoculturists who simply replace soiled substrate while ignoring the remainder of the enclosure are inviting problems.

Treatment. Treatment of mouth rot depends on the type and severity of the infection. If you plan to treat your boa yourself, you will need an assistant to hold the snake and keep its mouth pried open. In minor cases, infected tissues pull away very easily with little or no bleeding, leaving relatively healthy-looking tissue beneath. After cleaning the dead tissue away, rinse the area thoroughly with water and treat daily with Polysporin ointment. Neosporin can also be used, but contains less of the highly effective ingredient polymyxin B sulfate. In more serious and invasive cases, the infection goes much deeper. Affected tissues bleed easily and are not easily

removed. Treatment requires injections of antibiotics such as amikacin, subcutaneously and possibly into the gums themselves. Effective treatment could take several weeks, even months. Removal of affected tissue, and possibly even bone, makes this a condition more suitable for treatment by a qualified veterinarian.

Eye Infections

Although a snake's eyes are fairly well protected by the spectacles covering them, the fact that external parasites prefer to burrow around them plus the tendency of captive snakes to rub their heads along the glass surfaces of their enclosures make the eyes an entry point for bacteria. Symptoms to watch for include swelling in or around the eye, a cloudy appearance similar to pre-shedding yet only apparent in one eye, or the appearance of white or yellow pus under the spectacle. Immediate action by your veterinarian is required or the eye will be lost.

Dermatitis

Necrotizing dermatitis, also called *belly rot*, *scale rot*, or *blister disease*, is a progressive breakdown and ulceration of the skin and underlying tissues. Although this disease can occur anywhere on the skin, as the common name implies, it is most often seen on the ventral scales. Symptoms begin with a dark or rust-colored discoloration of the ventral scales, either in spots or as a long, continuous area.

Causes. The primary cause of dermatitis is maintaining a snake on consistently damp substrate, especially when combined with suboptimum cage temperatures and filthy enclosures. Avoid water dishes that can be tipped easily, and fill them only so far as to prevent overflowing when the snake soaks. Snakes that spend too much time soaking are also at risk. Except for the period just prior to shedding, and in the case of rainbow boas that appear to have a high resistance to dermatitis, do not allow your boa to remain in its dish excessively. Explore the possible reasons for this behavior—lack of a hide box, an excessively warm cage, external parasites, inadequate cage humidity—to determine if the habit can be broken. If not, prevent the snake from soaking by providing only a small water dish, or offering water for only a short period of time each day and removing it, preferably after dark if the snake does not prowl its cage during the day.

Prevention. Keeping your boa warm and dry, with expedient cleaning of the enclosure after defecation, should prevent this disease from ever appearing in your collection. With early detection and daily cleaning and treatment with Polysporin ointment, worked thoroughly into and under the scales of the affected area, minor cases can be stopped and reversed. Blisters will require draining before applying topical antibiotics. Serious cases are life-threatening, and require additional treatment with oral or injectable antibiotics.

Species Accounts: Central and South American Boas

Boa Constrictors—An Overview

The genus *Boa* currently contains a single species, *Boa constrictor*, the true boa constrictors. The taxonomy of boa constrictors poses many problems for taxonomists and serious collectors, and continues to be a subject of much debate. At the heart of the problem is not only determining which boas belong to which subspecies, but also whether some of those subspecies are even valid.

Subspecies

A number of subspecies are quite distinct in appearance and distribution so as to be generally accepted. On the mainland of South and Central America, these are the red-tail boa (*B. c. constrictor*), common boa (*B. c. imperator*), Argentine boa (*B. c. occidentalis*), and the Bolivian boa, also known as the Amaral's or short-tailed boa (*B. c. amarali*). Some other named forms, including Peruvian boas (*B. c. ortonii*), the Ecuadoran black-bellied boa (*B. c. melanogaster*), and the Mexican boa (*B. c. mexicana*), are now considered by some to be undeserving of subspecific status, but merely color variations of the common boa. The debate rages, and further additions, deletions, and reassignments are certain to occur in the future. A recent suggestion has been made that the Madagascan boas of the genus *Acrantophis* be moved into the genus *Boa*.

Island Boas

Several insular (island) forms of boa constrictors are also accepted as being correct, based on their unique characteristics and isolation from other populations. These include the clouded boa (*B. c. nebulosus*) from the island of Dominica in the West Indies; the Saboga Island boa (*B. c. sabogae*) from Saboga, near Panama; the St. Lucia boa (*B. c. orophias*) from St. Lucia; and *B. c. sigma* from the Tres Marias Islands. A small, light, and variably-colored form of common boa known as the Hog Island boa, from Cayos Cochinos off the Caribbean coast of Honduras, possibly extinct in the wild, is being seen more frequently in collections.

Most Common Boas

The two most common and popular forms of boa constrictors—the red-tails and the common boas—are also the source of the most confusion. Common boas, which are also referred to as Central American or Colombian boas, range from central Mexico through Central America and into northern and central South America. They are highly variable in pattern and coloration, and in habitat preference as well, ranging from lush jungles to semiarid scrub and rocky hillsides. The vast majority of boa constrictors imported into this country in the past and today are common boas, most of which originate in

The colorful Hog Island boa may be extinct in the wild.

Colombia. Most authorities agree that true red-tails originate only in the Amazon and Orinoco River basins of northern South America—eastern Peru, southern Colombia, Suriname, Guyana, and northern Brazil. Although red-tails are heavier-bodied and can grow to a larger size than common boas, the differences can often be subtle. Particularly attractive specimens of common boa are quite capable of displaying the trademark bright red colors of true red-tails, and many imported specimens labeled as red-tails are in fact just brightly colored common boas. The pet trade in boas has served to confuse the issue further, creating additional common names based on color or locality.

Serious breeders have long recognized that even within a well-defined species or subspecies, incompatibility between specimens from widely-separated locations is sometimes noted. The same can also be seen in specimens from different altitudes. The exact reasons are poorly understood, but may be related to incompatibility of reproductive organs or genes, or non-recognition of pheromones or courtship behaviors. In altitude-related incompatibility, the two snakes may have evolved to breed at entirely different times of the year, and may require different brumation strategies. Locality also gains importance when desirable colors or patterns are determined to be consistent within distinct populations. To meet the demand by breeders for more locality-specific animals, distributors began labeling red-tails with the country of origin, or in many cases, supposed origin, such as Guyana red-tails or Suriname red-tails. Although ostensibly a good idea, several new problems arose. First, many common boas with bright red tails shipped out of Colombia began to be labeled Colombian red-tails. Second, red-tails for which locality data is missing are often labeled on the questionable basis of color or pattern alone. Lastly, it must be suspected that some red-tails, and common boas as well, are being collected in countries that ban their exportation and smuggled into other countries that allow exportation.

Common Boa Constrictors (*Boa constrictor imperator*)

So, what kind of boa constrictor is right for you? For most herpeto-

Boa constrictors are highly variable in pattern and coloration, and in habitat preference.

culturists, the common boa is the best choice. They are much less expensive than red-tail boas, and yet superbly-colored and patterned specimens can be found with only a moderate amount of shopping around. As described throughout this book, both common boas and red-tails are extremely docile, excellent feeders on frozen-thawed rodents, and relatively simple to care for, so long as adequate space and temperature are provided. A possible exception is the northernmost population of common boas from Mexico, sometimes referred to as the Mexican boa (*B. c. mexicana*), a dark-colored form often considered to have a less than pleasant disposition.

As previously mentioned, common boas do not grow quite as long or heavy as do the red-tails. Adults will range in size from 6 to 9 feet (1.8–2.7 m), and are also considered easier to breed. Like other boa constrictors, spur size is a good indication of sex, being very conspicuous on males. The gestation period is four to eight months. Particularly large individuals are capable of producing 50 or more offspring, although the average is likely closer to 20 or 30. Neonates may be susceptible to cold or dehydration, but under warm, humid conditions will often readily accept small mice soon after birth. As with any baby snakes, neonates may be a bit nippy, but quicky calm down with regular handling.

Red-tail Boa Constrictors (*Boa constrictor constrictor*)

True red-tail boas set the standard by which all other boa constrictors are judged. Most are very light tan animals with sharp, bold saddles along the dorsum, that expand in width and turn to vivid red bordered with black on the anterior third of the snake. Heavier-bodied than common boas, adult red-tails may grow to a massive 12 to 14 feet (3.6–4.3 m) in length, although 9

A very attractive Peruvian red-tail boa constrictor.

to 10 feet (2.7–3 m) is more typical. Gestation and litter size are similar to those indicated for common boas. Due to their larger size, and the consensus that they are more difficult to breed in captivity and that multiple males may be required to induce courtship, breeding red-tails may be better suited to more advanced herpetoculturists. Of course, if you desire a truly beautiful boa and have the means to afford and house it, don't let this dissuade you from purchasing a red-tail. Just remember that adults will eventually require a 6- to 8-foot (1.8–2.4 m) cage, and feed on jumbo rats or even rabbits.

Bolivian Boa Constrictors (*Boa constrictor amarali*)

The Bolivian boa constrictor, also known as the Amaral's or short-tailed boa, is not as frequently available as other boa constrictors. Bolivian boas occupy a range between the red-tail boas to the north and the Argentine boas to the south, occurring from eastern Bolivia and Paraguay, eastward through southern Brazil to the coast. Color is variable, but similar to common and red-tail boas, although in this subspecies the posterior red saddles are typically seen only on the tail. Maximum size is relatively short, only about 6 to 7 feet (1.8–2.1 m). The tail is also shorter than on other boa constrictors. Care is similar to that for common boas.

Argentine Boa Constrictors (*Boa constrictor occidentalis*)

The Argentine boa constrictor is an unmistakable dark boa, patterned in dark brown or black. It represents the southernmost race of boa constrictor, occurring in northern Argentina, southeastern Bolivia and portions of Paraguay, and is listed as a CITES Appendix I species. Juveniles may display dorsal patches of pink or brown that typically also darken as the animal matures. Adults can grow to 7 to 9 feet (2.1–2.7 m). Argentines may readily exhibit the defensive posture of gaping the mouth at intruders and hissing very loudly. In my experience with a limited number of captive-bred specimens, this threatening behavior has been entirely bluff. However, to say that an Argentine boa's bark is worse than its bite would remain true only so long as there is no bite. If you can bring yourself to ignore the threat and handle the snake regularly, this behavior quickly disappears.

Argentine boas are attractive animals, and with proper handling can

Despite its reputation for bad temper, Argentine boa constrictors can become as docile as their more northern relatives.

become as docile as other more widely-kept forms. Due to their southern origins, this species may require somewhat cooler temperatures to induce breeding. They should not be subjected to constant cool temperatures that can result in serious respiratory infections. An eight-week period of cycling, using a nighttime low temperature of 60 to 65°F (15.6–18°C) and a daytime high in the low 80s F (26.7–29°C), is a much better and safer approach. Argentines may not breed until after cooling has been suspended, rather than during cooling as with other boa constrictors. Gestation lasts approximately six months. Litter size may exceed 40.

Insular Boa Constrictors (*Boa c. nebulosus, B. c. sabogae, B. c. orophias*)

Insular forms of boa constrictors are less common in collections than their mainland relatives. Although generally smaller in size, they tend to exhibit darker coloration and subdued pattern. Some, like the clouded boa (*B. c. nebulosus*), are also known for having nasty dispositions. The relative scarcity of the insular forms serves to keep prices higher than for many other species. Herpetoculturists who keep them have often maintained other boas first, and do so for the additional challenge involved or to expand or complete their understanding of this fascinating group of snakes. With the increased threat of extinction to island species, the efforts of these breeders are to be commended.

Rainbow Boas (*Epicrates cenchria*)

As many as nine subspecies of rainbow boas have been identified, occurring throughout much of South America and on a handful of its coastal islands. Members of this species can grow to 5 to 7 feet

(1.5–2.1 m) and are fairly similar in habits. All are patterned with a series of dark circles or large spots on the dorsum and sides, on a solid background in some shade of red or brown. The background coloration may fade at night, particularly on the sides, to nearly pure white. Their skin displays a high level of iridescence when exposed to the sun or other bright light, giving them their common name. A series of heat-sensitive pits can be found in the upper and lower labial scales, aiding the species in locating warm-blooded prey.

The majority of subspecies are rare in collections. The attractively-colored Brazilian rainbow boa (*E. c. cenchria*) of Suriname, Guyana, southern Venezuela, and Brazil, is by far the most commonly seen in collections. Exceptional specimens have a background color of dark orange to blood-red. The dorsal pattern is a single row of often perfectly circular black rings. A row of uniformly large, black spots, each containing a single, bright orange or yellow horizontal crescent near the top, adorns the sides. Smaller numbers of the drably-colored Colombian rainbow boa (*E. c. maurus*), a northern form found as far north as Costa Rica, and an even smaller number of Argentine rainbow boas (*E. c. alvarezi*) are also kept and occasionally bred in captivity. The remaining forms include the Peruvian rainbow boa (*E. c. gaigei*), a beautiful form found in Peru and Bolivia that rivals the Brazilians in coloration, as well as *E. c. crassus* from Argentina, Brazil, and Paraguay, *E. c. barbouri* from Marajo Island off Brazil, and three additional forms all found in Brazil—*E. c. polylepsis*, *E. c. hygrophilus*, and *E. c. assisi*.

Temperament and Care

With moderate interaction and handling, rainbow boas can become docile pets. They are extremely powerful con-

The iridescence that gives rainbow boas their name can be seen clearly in this Brazilian rainbow boa.

strictors, often wrapping tightly around the hands and arms when removed from their cage. A cage temperature of mid-80s F (26.7–29°C) during the day and mid 70s F (21–24°C) at night is ideal. Colombians may prefer slightly higher temperatures. High humidity is important, especially for Brazilians, and they should be observed for signs of dehydration. Regurgitation, poor skin condition, and difficulty in shedding are symptoms of low humidity. A large water dish or tub should be provided to help increase humidity levels and allow the snake to soak. Some specimens

Less colorful than the Brazilians, Argentine rainbow boas are nevertheless intricately patterned.

Typical pale coloration of juvenile Brazilian rainbow boas. With adults ranging from an unpopular brown to the coveted bright orange "Lamar" phase, smart collectors will ask about the parents before buying.

will be seen soaking regularly, while others may never soak, even when maintained under identical conditions. Rainbow boas have a high level of resistance to dermatitis, or blister disease (see page 61), and can be allowed to soak for long periods with less concern than would be appropriate for other species. However, for a snake that soaks day and night, try increasing the overall cage humidity by reducing cage ventilation and lightly misting the enclosure and inside of the hide box daily with water.

Breeding strategy for rainbow boas is similar to common boa constrictors, dropping nighttime temperatures into the low 70s F (21–24°C), with associated daytime highs in the 80s F (26.7–29°C). Argentines, being the more southerly race, may require slightly lower temperatures. The gestation period is four to eight months. Litters can number as high as 30, although Argentines produce fewer, but larger offspring. All are excellent feeders on small mice. Neonate Brazilians and Colombians are born with lighter background coloration, assuming their adult shades of brown or red during their first year or two.

This can make buying juveniles for future color-specific breeding projects a bit of a gamble.

Insular *Epicrates*

In addition to the mainland *Epicrates cenchria*, ten additional forms of the genus are found on islands throughout the Caribbean. Some species have been divided into two or more subspecies, usually with home islands of their own. The small size of many of these islands, combined with growing pressures from human population, agriculture, tourism development, and introduced predators such as the mongoose have pushed some of these species to the brink of extinction. None of the insular *Epicrates* are particularly common in collections, which is unfortunate. Captive populations may soon be all that remains.

Four insular species of *Epicrates* grow to moderate sizes, with the largest being the Cuban boa (*E. angulifer*) at up to 12 feet (3.65 m). The others, capable of achieving lengths of 6 to 8 feet (1.8–2.4 m), are the Jamaican boa (*E. subflavus*), Puerto Rican boa (*E. inornatus*), and the Haitian boa (*E. striatus*), of which eight subspecies can be found on several islands. As juveniles they tend to be arboreal, searching for lizards as prey, but become more terrestrial as their size increases. The Jamaican and Puerto Rican forms are endangered, and listed as Appendix I animals by CITES. The Puerto Rican boa's specific name of *inornatus*, translated to "not ornate," might be said to apply to the group as a whole. Bright colors are not the norm, but while *inornatus* is indeed a dark snake with only a faintly discernable pattern, the others are attractive, shiny animals with dark, ragged crossbands on a light and occasionally bright background of red, yellow, gray, or brown.

The remaining six species of *Epicrates* are even less commonly

Cuban boas, the largest of the Caribbean boas, can grow to 12 feet.

The Caicos Island boa (E. chrysogaster) *exists as both a blotched and a boldly striped phase.*

Eight subspecies of the Haitian boa can be found on several islands. This is the Cat Island Boa (Epicrates striatus ailurus).

The endangered Jamaican boa. Population growth and development for tourism has put many such island boas at risk.

seen in collections. They are *E. chrysogaster*, *E. relicquus*, *E. fordi*, *E. exsul*, *E. gracilis*, and *E. monensis*. The last form is also a CITES Appendix I animal. All are much smaller and more slender snakes, with body shape more closely resembling the rat snakes, and spend more time in trees and shrubs than do the larger forms. Coloration consists of dark spots, blotches, or crossbands, usually on a drab background of gray to brown. At least one species, *E. chryso-gaster*, exists as both a blotched and a boldly striped phase.

Care and Breeding

Captive care for *Epicrates* is fairly uniform. Moderately warm temperatures and branches for climbing should be provided. Spacious enclosures have been suggested for the larger forms. No humidity requirements are noted, although high humidity may be helpful in eliciting courtship behavior. Various species are reported to breed easily using nighttime temperature drops, misting with water, and the use of multiple males. Many, however, appear to be only biennial breeders. Litter size varies by species. Jamaican boas may produce up to 40 offspring, and Haitian and Puerto Rican boas as many as 25. All others typically produce a dozen or fewer. The young may prefer lizards, but can be switched to newborn mice by scenting them with a lizard.

Emerald Tree Boas (*Corallus caninus*)

Emerald tree boas are some of the most unique and fascinating animals of the reptile world. As the name implies, the overall adult color is a pale to sometimes stunning emerald green. Juveniles may be bright red, red-orange, or brown, with small patches of green that spread over the entire body during their first year. The only pattern present may be a thin white stripe along the spine, and/or a series of thin, white bands or half-bands, as if white paint had been dripped on the spine and trickled down. Labial and ventral scales are white or yellow. The large head is made even more

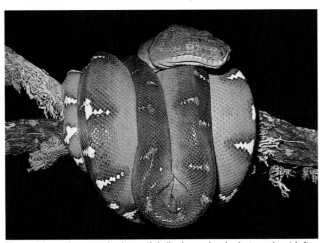

Emerald tree boas make beautiful display animals, but are best left to experienced keepers.

pronounced by an extremely slender neck. Adults can exceed 6 feet (1.8 m) in length. Inhabiting lush rainforests of northern South America, the species is primarily arboreal, occasionally exploring the forest floor during nocturnal hunting. In the wild, they feed on a variety of small mammals, bats, and birds. Rows of extremely pronounced heat-sensitive pits in the upper and lower labial scales and exceptionally long, curved teeth give these snakes the ability to snatch hapless birds and bats right out of flight, although their nocturnal ways may mean that sleeping birds make up much of the diet. Juveniles feed on lizards and frogs as well.

Emeralds are perhaps best known for their trademark resting pose, tightly curled up on a horizontal tree branch or a Y-shaped fork, with the head resting comfortably in the middle. They achieve this pose by circling the body along the top of the branch in increasingly smaller circles until the body is tightly bunched. A strong but not excessively thick branch is usually chosen, so that, as the coils settle in front and back, they meet underneath the branch, providing a secure hold against wind or predators. Emerald tree boas often remain motionless in this position throughout the day, becoming active only after nightfall. If bothered in the resting pose, they may choose to bury their head in their coils rather than bite. The coils may also serve to collect rainwater for drinking.

Amazon Basin Emeralds

Although no subspecies are currently identified, hobbyists generally recognize a separate phase, commonly referred to as Amazonian or Amazon Basin emeralds. These tend to be longer and heavier-bodied, with a deep, dark green color, brilliant yellow labial and ventral scales, and a solid white stripe along the spine. Amazon Basin emeralds are also reported by some keepers to be quite docile. Maintaining either phase is best left to serious and experienced herpetoculturists. Although exceptionally beautiful display animals, emeralds can exhibit nasty dispositions and cannot be considered good pets. This is not to say that they can't become docile with regular handling, but this entails an almost daily struggle urging or prying them off their perch, with its inherent risk of getting bitten and of stress or injury to the snake. One look at an emerald's huge teeth is enough to convince most hobbyists that being bitten is going to hurt, and hurt a lot! Not long ago I purchased a pair of docile emeralds, but failed to handle them frequently. The female subsequently bit me on the back of the head during handling. I no longer keep emeralds.

Care of Emeralds

If you're up to the challenge, emeralds require a large vertical cage with plenty of strong horizontal branches or perches. Provide a daytime temperature gradient by placing a spotlight or ceramic heat lamp over one end of the highest perch. High relative humidity is important, so include a large water dish or tub and control ventilation. Daily misting with water may be required, especially during the shedding cycle. Some keepers mount additional water dishes to the side of tall enclosures near preferred basking spots, to help ensure adequate hydration. Emeralds are susceptible to respiratory illness and also a regurgitation syndrome, in which the animal consistently cannot hold down food. The underlying causes may be low humidity or temperature, or something more insidious. Isolate ill specimens using optimum conditions immediately.

Emeralds are sedentary creatures, that should only be fed small meals biweekly. Defecation is infrequent, and feeding should be halted if too much time elapses. Regularly-spaced feeding

Juvenile emerald tree boas may be red, orange, brown, or green.

and careful record keeping can alert you to problems. Soaking the snake in a tub of lukewarm water will often resolve impactions. Frozen-thawed rodents are readily accepted as prey, particularly when offered slightly warm. As mentioned in the section on feeding (beginning on page 34), avoid overheating rodents. Feeding is best when attempted at night, after the snake has begun to wake up, and when food is offered from below using long forceps. Daytime attempts at feeding often result in the snake simply burying its head. Newly imported specimens may be difficult feeders, refusing to eat or preferring fowl or live prey. Males are reported to occasionally go off feed for several months. Reluctant feeders may be enticed to strike by offering a rodent from above while pinching the snake lightly from below, or you can try leaving a live or stunned prey animal on the cage floor for the snake to observe and seize from above. Constriction and swallowing are accomplished while hanging from a perch.

Breeding Emeralds

Breeding success for emerald tree boas is growing in frequency. This is

Amazon tree boas are extremely variable in color, and noted for their unpleasant dispositions.

encouraging news, as their unique requirements makes the importation process tough on them. Captive-bred juveniles appear to exhibit far fewer difficulties than imports. Breeding is achieved as with other boas, by lowering nighttime temperatures to near 70°F (21°C), with associated daytime temperatures in the mid-80s F (26.7–29°C) for a period of four to six weeks before placing the male and female together. Seasonal variation in humidity—high in summer and somewhat lower in winter—with heavy misting during passing low-pressure storm fronts, may help imitate the natural conditions and induce breeding. Copulation occurs arboreally, with the tails entwined and hanging below the pair. The gestation period is five to seven months, with 6 to 20 offspring being born in August to October. Neonates seem to prefer fuzzy mice as first foods. Most breeders maintain neonates in small glass jars or plastic boxes, with an inch of water on the bottom and a secure perch. The humidity and nightly swims serve the snakes well during their first year.

Tree Boas (*Corallus enydris*), Annulated Boas (*Corallus annulatus*)

The other species of the genus *Corallus* are similar to the emerald tree boa in their arboreal habits and preferences, but much more slender in build. They also rest curled up in trees, although not with the neatness of the emeralds. The eyes are quite large, aiding in nocturnal hunting. Coloration in both species is extremely variable, and several color phases may be produced within a single litter.

The Amazon tree boa (*C. enydris enydris*) ranges throughout the Amazon basin, while the Cook's tree boa (*C. e. cooki*) inhabits the islands of Grenada, Trinidad, St. Vincent, Union, and Curacao. Coloration ranges from a

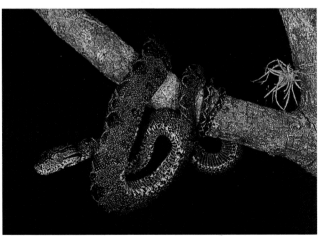

"Garden phase" Amazon tree boa. Several color phases may occur in a single litter.

uniform beige, brown, yellow, orange, or red, to heavily speckled or patterned.

The three South American subspecies of the annulated boa are also restricted in range—*C. annulatus annulatus* in south central areas, *C. a. colombianus* in Colombia, and *C. a. brombergi* in Ecuador. Color and pattern consist of faded dark oblong rings laterally, on a background of bright red, dark orange, or black.

Tree and annulated boas are not regularly maintained in captivity except by experienced hobbyists, with the Amazon tree boa being the most commonly kept of the group. Although colorful, all are noted for their unpleasant dispositions. Care and breeding are similar to that for emerald tree boas, although Amazon tree boas may be late spring breeders (Ross and Marzec, 1990). Offspring can number as many as 15. Neonates may initially require lizards or frogs as prey.

Cook's tree boa.

Anacondas (*Eunectes*)

Although five species of anacondas, occasionally referred to as "water boas," have been or are in the process of being identified taxonomically, only the green (*E. murinus*) and the yellow (*E. notaeus*) anacondas are generally seen in captivity. Inhabiting lush tropical rain forests of South America, the green anaconda is an olive green to grayish snake, with small black oval spots. Large specimens often measure 12 to 20 feet (3.65–6 m) in length, and are capable of exceeding 30 feet (9 m). Although the reticulated python may grow longer, the green anaconda's huge girth makes it the world's most massive snake. The yellow anaconda is much smaller in length and girth, growing to 10 to 12 feet (3–3.65 m) or more. The pattern of dark blotches is noticeably more dense than its green relative, on a background of bright to pale yellow. It has a smaller range, occurring in southern areas of the Amazon basin. All species spend a great deal of time submerged in swamps and sluggish rivers, providing them with protection, ease of movement, and concealment for ambushing prey. Birds, mammals, turtles, and even caimans (reptiles similar to alligators)

Annulated boa.

The enormous size and bad temper of green anacondas makes them unsuitable as pets.

are taken. Juveniles may include fish in the diet.

Due to their enormous size and tendency for bad temperament, only a limited number of yellow anacondas and even fewer green anacondas are kept in collections. Large enclosures with a suitable water pool are required. Copulation and even birth of the offspring typically take place in water.

Smaller than its green relative, yellow anacondas may still reach 12 feet.

The number and size of neonates varies with the size of the female.

Tropidophid Boas (*Tropidophis, Ungaliophis, Trachyboa, Exiliboa*)

These four genera are poorly understood and rarely seen in collections. All are short snakes. Cloacal spurs are typically absent or hidden in females. McDowell (1987) and Kluge (1991) place this group into their own family, apart from the true boids. They will likely continue to be debated on taxonomic grounds for some time to come, and are mentioned here for reference only.

Fifteen species and many more subspecies of the secretive dwarf boa (*Tropidophis*), also referred to as wood snakes, occur from western South America to Brazil and on a number of Caribbean islands. Dwarf boas, as the name implies, are a small species, growing to about 3 feet (.9 m). Their diet includes lizards, frogs, small mammals, and birds. Coloration is generally brown or gray, with a pattern of slightly darker, paired spots along the dorsum. Several forms are reported to lighten in color at night. An unusual defensive adaptation is the ability to rupture blood vessels in the eyes and mouth when provoked.

The two species of Central American dwarf boas (*Ungaliophis*), also known as banana or bromeliad boas, are attractive snakes found in southern Mexico (*U. continentalis*), and from southeastern Panama southward to northern Colombia (*U. panamensis*). Coloration consists of paired, black oval or triangular spots ringed with a thin border of white or brown, on a gray to brown background. Both species are secretive and arboreal. Adults grow to only about 30 inches (76 cm), and feed on lizards, frogs, small mammals, and birds. They are rare in captivity, and erratic feeders.

Banana, or bromeliad, boas are rarely seen in collections. This is the form from southern Mexico (Ungaliophus continentalis).

The rough-scaled or eyelash boa (*Trachyboa boulengeri* of Panama, Colombia and Ecuador, and *T. gularis* of western Ecuador) are short, stout snakes with a very un-boa-like look. The scales are heavily keeled, with the scales of the head protruding to give the snake a spiked appearance. Coloration is an overall dark red-brown, black, and gray. Most likely a terrestrial or semiarboreal species, eyelash boas are reported to feed on fish or amphibians.

The rare Oaxaca boa (*Exiliboa placata*) is a fairly recently discovered glossy black snake found near Oaxaca, Mexico. Few specimens have been collected and very little is known about the species.

Xenoboas

Xenoboa cropanii is known from only three specimens found near Sao Paulo, Brazil, and is believed to now be extinct. Kluge (1991) reclassifies *Xenoboa cropanii* as *Corallus cropanii*.

Species Accounts: North American Boas

Rosy Boas (*Lichanura trivirgata*)

The rosy boas are one of only two species of boas that occur naturally in the United States. They are a group of colorfully striped, diminutive snakes, rarely exceeding 2 to 3 feet (.61–.9 m) in length. Several subspecies are currently recognized, although the validity of some are in question. Rosy boas inhabit sandy and rocky desert areas of southern California, western and southern Arizona, southward into Baja and northwestern Mexico. The species name, *trivirgata*, meaning "three stripes," is descriptive of the typical pattern, as most subspecies have three thick, evenly spaced stripes running the entire length of the body. Coastal rosy boas (*L. t. roseofusca*) of coastal northern Baja and extreme southern California are the exception, often having stripes being so close to the background coloration as to produce a unicolor appearance. The dorsal stripe begins at the nose, while the lateral stripes begin at the eyes, which may be colored to match. Stripe colors vary by subspecies in thickness, evenness, and color, ranging from the orange or bright red of desert rosy boas (*L. t. gracia*) and mid-Baja rosy boas (*L. t. myriolepis* or *L. t. saslowi*, depending on the authority) to chocolate-brown or black in the Mexican rosy boa (*L. t. trivirgata*) of southern Baja, northwestern Mexico (Sonora), and southcentral Arizona. The background and ventral surface is typically a light shade of slate gray, cream, or tan. All rosy boas are similar in build. The tapered head is small and indistinctive from the neck, an adaptation common to burrowing snakes. The cylindrical body is short, yet stout, with an unusually soft or "squishy" feel. The tail is short and blunt. Subspecific determination is made based on locality, scale counts, coloration, and stripe characteristics.

In the wild, local populations of rosy boas may be quite variable in coloration, even within a subspecies. Small rocky outcroppings or canyons surrounded by open desert sands can serve to isolate a population as effectively as an ocean-locked island. As with many other variable species of snakes, a number of serious collectors and breeders have begun labeling rosy boas with locality-specific names, in order to preserve color, genetic, and behavioral traits that may have evolved within a particular population. This should make taxonomists and biologists ecstatic, or at least permit them to exclaim a smug "I told you so!," considering that their primary beef against captive breeding has always been that

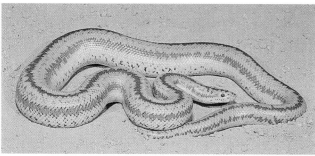

Desert rosy boa. Small and docile, rosy boas are an excellent choice for a first snake.

animals without specific locality data are scientifically useless for many types of research, and certainly for reintroduction into the wild. Taxonomists however, are currently occupied with other aspects of rosy boa classification, arguing the validity of certain subspecies and the boundaries of others. For example, Spiteri (1987) and some others now consider the mid-Baja peninsula population (commonly labeled the mid-Baja rosy boa, *L. t. myriolepis*) to be *L. t. saslowi*, with *L. t. myriolepis* occurring not in Baja but in southern California and eastward to Arizona, replacing *L. t. gracia*. Spiteri also proposes that the western Arizona population be given subspecific status as *L. t. arizonae*, instead of *L. t. myriolepis*. The suggestion has even been made (Kluge, 1993) that the entire *Lichanura* group should be blended into *Charina*. Regardless of the final outcome, locality-specific breeding represents a positive step forward for herpetoculturists, provided that identification is based on the known collection site of an animal or its progenitors, and not on fallible color or pattern generalities.

Typical desert rosy boa habitat in southern California's Joshua Tree National Monument.

Description and Care

Rosy boas are docile, low-maintenance captives, which, when combined with moderate prices, attractive coloration, and small size, makes them ideal pets. All are quite uniform in their captive requirements. They are active snakes that do a fair share of climbing, and yet do well in small cages. A large number can be maintained in a very small area by utilizing a rack-type system of pull-out boxes. Attractive rack systems, complete with prewired lights and heating elements, are commercially available and regularly advertised in herpetoculture magazines (see pages 89–90). Low relative humidity and excellent ventilation are a must. Include only a very small water dish of a type that is unlikely to be tipped over. Some keepers offer water only for a short period of time once or twice weekly, in order to reduce the humidity level and the possibility of spills. Rosy boas seem to prefer temperatures in the low 80s F (26.7–29°C), and may take to the water dish when temperatures exceed 85°F (29°C). In my experience, which is limited to *L. t. saslowi*, regurgitation is common if daytime highs fail to reach 80°F (26.7°C). Pine and aspen shavings can be used as substrate to satisfy their urge to burrow, but newspaper works equally well and is easier to keep clean. A snug hide box or hollow tube should also be provided. As an adaptation to their harsh desert life, rosy boas seem especially adept at converting excess food into fat, and care should be exercised to prevent them from becoming obese. Small food items are preferred over large ones. Feeding one or two small mice once a week is sufficient, but cut back if the snake appears lumpy along the ventral or lateral surfaces.

Breeding

Rosy boas are extremely easy to breed. Adults are springtime breeders,

Mid-Baja rosy boas typically have even orange stripes.

and can sometimes be bred after their second winter, although much better short- and long-term results are achieved by waiting until after the third winter. Best results occur after an 8 to 12 week period of cooling into the upper 50s F (13–15°C) or low 60s F (16.1–18°C), although some breeders don't cool their animals at all. I have had success leaving them in a garage that fluctuated wildly during Florida's hot and cold spells from 54 to 78°F (12–25.6°C) from December through February, warming them back up in

Gravid female Mexican rosy boa.

early March. Because rosy boas would naturally deal with cold weather by going underground, I do not utilize any additional lighting beyond the small amount finding its way around the garage door. After brumation, resume normal feeding for males and heavier feeding for females. Introduce pairs beginning in early April. Leaving them together, with occasional short separations, can improve the chance of successful copulation. Breeding typically occurs in April through June. A pronounced increase in girth leaves little doubt when the female is gravid. Females may cruise the cage incessantly if a warm basking site of 87 to 90°F (30.5–32°C) is not provided. The gestation period is four to six months. Small litters are the norm, usually numbering four to ten offspring.

Neonates

As with other boas, neonate rosy boas should be observed for signs of dehydration prior to their first shedding. Pinkies are often accepted as the first food. Some neonates may refuse food until their first spring. If all feeding tricks fail, some breeders suggest cooling the neonates as if for breeding, and trying again after the spring warm-up. I recently tried this with three neonate *L. t. saslowi*, resulting in one death and one near-death within two weeks. The bad results may have been related to too-cool temperatures (dipping to 52°F [11°C] one night), failure to drink, or inadequate yolk/fat reserves (the neonates were three months old). One successful rosy boa breeder consulted for this book suggests that Mexican rosy boas are often difficult to induce feeding, and that neonates are sometimes cooled into the low 60s F (15.6–18°C) for a one month "mini-brumation" immediately after their first shed. Other suggestions included changing substrates, using older pinkies instead of newborns, and even giving the neonates a rough ride in your car.

Rubber Boas (*Charina bottae*)

Rubber boas, of which three sub-species are recognized or debated, are the second species of boa found in the United States, occurring from southern California, east as far as Utah and Montana, and as far north as British Columbia, Canada. The form is patternless and quite shiny, being a nearly uniform shade of beige to dark brown or olive. Unlike most other boas, this species has large symmetrical plates instead of small scales on the top of the head. Adults seldom exceed 2 feet (.61 m) in length. These snakes spend much of their time burrowing in humid, loose soil or rotting logs in search of small rodents and amphibians. Birds are occasionally taken. The tail is blunt and rounded, mimicking the head. A common defensive strategy is to gather the body into a tight ball with the head protected inside, while offering the tail up to a potential predator.

Rubber boas are seldom kept by hobbyists due to their secretive nature and dull color. They prefer temperatures substantially cooler than other boas. Daytime highs in the 70s F (21–26°C) and nighttime lows that drop into the 60s F (15.6–20.6°C) or even 50s F (10–15°C) seem to pose no problems. Wood shavings or mulch are acceptable substrates. The typical

Rubber boas are rarely kept in captivity. Note the blunt tail.

boa fare of small rodents make up the diet. Much of the rubber boa's range receives freezing temperatures and snow during winter, making the species a spring breeder. Breeding them in captivity requires much cooler temperatures than for other boas, with nighttime lows approaching 55°F (12.8°C). Reduce or eliminate lighting during brumation. Breeding typically occurs in April or May, with offspring being born in August and on into September. Small litters of three to eight are typical, and neonates are reported to be difficult to initiate feeding. Successful breeding may not be possible on an annual basis.

Species Accounts: Old World Boas

Overview

Boas are primarily New World snakes. However, a few Old World species do exist and have been growing in popularity in recent years. For those who enjoy the thought of owning a boa, but who choose not to deal with large snakes, a small, yet colorful boa that eats mice (as opposed to lizards) has great appeal. Such is the case with the sand boas of Africa and Southwestern Asia, an expanding group introduced fairly recently to herpetoculturists.

Rain forest habitat of the Madagascar tree boa. Madagascar's natural resources are under severe human pressure.

Interest in the snakes of Madagascar, an island country off the southeast African coast, may have come in the nick of time, if not a bit too late. About 90 percent of Madagascar's animals, including a number of unique snakes and lizards, and 80 percent of its plants are endemic, occurring nowhere else on earth. Unfortunately, the island is facing the typical problems associated with a burgeoning population. Deforestation caused by lumbering, slash-and-burn farming, and unrestricted cattle grazing has been devastating. While the government has made serious efforts to protect some of its remaining critical habitats, it remains to be seen what the future holds. Madagascan boas of the genus *Acrantophis* and *Sanzinia* are listed as Appendix I species by CITES. Madagascar currently prohibits their export, making continued propagation of the small number of specimens already in private collections problematic. Maintaining genetic diversity is difficult when most owners have no idea of the lineage of their boas. Responsible owners of these attractive Madagascar species should make every effort to avoid further inbreeding.

Madagascar's boas, like so many other boas, are currently undergoing taxonomic scrutiny. Both species of *Acrantophis* closely resemble common boa constrictors in overall appearance and gentle demeanor, and there has been suggestion (Kluge, 1991) that both *Acrantophis* and *Sanzinia* should be placed into the genus *Boa*. Because the Madagascar ground boa (*A. madagascariensis*) and Madagascar tree boa (*S. madagascariensis*) share the same species name *madagascariensis*, Kluge recommends *Boa madagascariensis* for the former and *Boa mandrita* for the latter. The Dumeril's boa (*A. dumerili*) would of course become *Boa dumerili*.

Dumeril's Boas (*Acrantophis dumerili*) and Madagascar Ground Boas (*Acrantophis madagascariensis*)

Although the Madagascar ground boa is infrequently seen in collections, the Dumeril's boa is much more common and can be found on many price lists and at reptile shows. In the wild, the Dumeril's boa occupies the south and southwest portions of the island, while the ground boa inhabits the north and east. Similar in appearance, both species of *Acrantophis* are relatively large, heavy-bodied ground-dwellers. A mottled pattern of browns, tans, and black provides excellent camouflage when lying in leaf litter. Particularly attractive specimens exhibit large amounts of pink or copper coloration.

Both species do very well in captivity following maintenance and breeding techniques similar to common boa constrictors. Ground boas can grow to be 8 to 10 feet (2–3 m) in length, yet they produce relatively small numbers of large offspring, typically fewer than 10. Although smaller in length and girth, with an adult size of only 6 to 7 feet (1.8–2.1 m), litter sizes for Dumeril's boas can exceed 20 neonates. Dumeril's boas are considered easier to breed. The gestation period for Dumeril's boas is approximately seven months, and eight to nine months for ground boas. If you would like a relatively large boa, yet are daunted by the thought of owning

Slightly smaller but with all the positive attributes of boa constrictors, the Dumeril's boa is gaining in popularity.

an 8- to 10-foot (2–3 m) snake, I highly recommend Dumeril's boas as an option to the larger common or red-tail boa constrictors.

Madagascar Tree Boas (*Sanzinia madagascariensis*)

The Madagascar tree boa is the single representative of the genus *Sanzinia*. An attractive boa, it still remains somewhat uncommon in

Madagascar ground boa. Although larger than the Dumeril's boa, ground boas have fewer offspring.

Madagascar tree boas may not be as arboreal as their common name implies.

collections. *Sanzinia* may not be as arboreal as its common name implies, as specimens are often found in terrestrial locations. Adults can reach 6 to 7 feet (1.8–2.1 m) in length. Neonates

Juvenile Madagascar tree boa.

may be born red, acquiring the adult coloration of green or grayish-green during their first year. Some individuals from northern areas are yellowish. The skin is highly iridescent, with a bold pattern of irregular dark triangles traced with white alternating down the back, sometimes meeting to form hour-glass-shaped bands. As with many other arboreal and semiarboreal boas, *Sanzinia* has conspicuous heat-sensitive pits among the labial scales. They are nocturnal hunters, feeding on birds, bats, and small mammals in the wild.

Madagascar tree boas are reported to be fairly calm in captivity. While some sources suggest captive care similar to that of the emerald tree boa, with vertical space and climbing opportunities, I know of at least one breeder who maintains the species in large blanket boxes on a rack system. Breeding may be achieved by placing snakes together and dropping the daytime and nighttime temperatures several degrees for a period of two months. Females grow noticeably darker when gravid, an adaptation that allows for increased heat absorption. Gestation is six to eight months, and the average litter size is six to sixteen. The young will usually accept very small mice.

Sand Boas (*Eryx*)

Sand boas represent a growing group—11 or more species and several subspecies—of very small, burrowing boas, inhabiting arid and rocky habitats from northern Africa east to Pakistan and India. Despite their wide dispersal, they are quite similar in appearance and habits. The eyes are placed high on a wedge-shaped head. The tail is very blunt, making it difficult for predators, and sometimes herpetoculturists, to tell at a glance which end is the head. The dorsal pattern typically consists of irregular dark brown or black blotches, or "splatters," in a single row along the spine or along both sides, sometimes forming an unbroken but jagged stripe. The background is pale to bright yellow, orange, tan, or gray. Pattern and coloration sometimes begins at the neck, leaving the head gray or beige and unpatterned except for a dark diagonal stripe through the eyes. Amelanistic (lacking black) or anerythristic (lacking red) color morphs can be found. The smooth-scaled sand boas begin life with faint bands but fade to a uniform brown as the snake grows. The ventral surface is pale colored and unpatterned.

Care

Adult sand boas rarely achieve 3 feet (.9 m) in length, with adult females growing significantly longer and heavier than adult males. With adequate handling, they can become quite docile, and their small size makes them suitable pets for almost any keeper. They are fossorial and nocturnal in the wild, and in captivity will spend most of their time in hiding. A popular and natural choice for substrate is washed sand (avoid silica-based beach sand) to a depth of about 3 inches (7.6 cm), into which the snakes can burrow. Wood chips, aspen bedding, and newspaper are also suitable. A hide box is not necessary if the snake is able to burrow under the substrate. If newspaper is used, provide several layers for the snake to hide between, in order to keep it off the less sterile cage floor, as well as a small hide box. Good ventilation and a small water dish that is hard to spill are also necessary to keep humidity low. If a rack system is being used, the boxes should have ample holes drilled on all four sides. Further reduction of humidity can be accomplished by offering water only at night, two or three times per week. An under-tank heating pad at one end of the cage, or heating cable for a rack system, is recommended. If frozen-thawed mice are offered but refused, try live mice. Sand boas often wait in ambush just below the surface for prey to walk by.

Common Types

The most common types kept in captivity are the Egyptian sand boa (*E. colubrinus colubrinus*), Kenyan or East African sand boa (*E. c. loveridgei*), rough-scaled sand boa (*E. conicus conicus*), and smooth-scaled sand boa (*E. johnii*). Some taxonomists place the rough-scaled sand boa in its own genus, *Gongylophis*. Other species include *E. jaculus, E. elegans, E. jayakari, E. miliaris, E. muelleri, E. nogaiorum, E. somalicus,* and *E. tartaricus*. Many species include one or more additional subspecies.

Breeding

Sand boas have been successfully bred as early as 14 months of age, although most will first breed in their second or third spring. Successful breeding has been achieved without winter cooling, although some breeders prefer to cool their sand boas into the low to mid-60s F (16–18°C) for a period of several weeks, and others drop the nighttime temperature to

Egyptian sand boa.

Kenyan sand boa. Sand boas will spend much of their time buried under the substrate.

near 70°F (21.1°C) with a daytime high around 80°F (26.7°C). These snakes often copulate while the female or even both snakes remain buried in the sand, with the tails protruding out of the sand at a 90-degree angle. Gestation averages from four to six months, and gravid females often take advantage of a basking site in excess of 95°F (35°C). The number of neonates varies by species, with maximum litter size typically being 12 to 30. Offering neonates several newborn mice at night will increase the likelihood of one being found and eaten. Some sand boas may not breed every year.

Species Accounts: Pacific Boas

Pacific Boas (*Candoia*)

Three species of small to moderate-sized boas inhabit a number of South Pacific islands, including New Guinea, Fiji, and the Solomons. Where their home ranges overlap, the different habitat preferences of *Candoia* allow them to successfully coexist. All have keeled scales and a flat, angled rostral scale giving the appearance of a sharply pointed snout when viewed from the side. Far removed geographically from other types of boas, the ancestors of these snakes likely arrived on current-driven rafts of vegetation from South America, a theory supported by the additional presence on Fiji of relatives of the green iguana.

The largest and most arboreal species of *Candoia* is the Fiji boa (*C. bibroni bibroni*), a slender, 5- to 6-foot (1.5–1.8 m) snake of the Fiji, Samoan, Solomon, New Hebrides, and Loyalty islands. One subspecies, the Solomon Islands tree boa (*C. b. australis*), is recognized. Occupying the middle ground is the semiarboreal Indonesian or Pacific ground boa (*C. carinata carinata*), a slender, 2- to 3-foot (.6–.9 m) snake occurring on New Guinea, the Solomons, and surrounding islands. One additional subspecies, the Solomon Islands ground boa (*C. c. paulsoni*), is recognized. The viper boa (*C. aspera*), a short, stocky mimic of the death adder (*Acanthophis*), rounds out the trio. This species is a ground-dweller, also of New Guinea, the Bismarck archipelago, and surrounding islands. Adults grow to just over 3 feet (.9 m). In the wild, all three species feed on small mammals, lizards, frogs, and occasionally birds.

C. bibroni and *C. carinata* are highly variable in coloration and pattern. *C. bibroni* may be pale brown, gray, or red, heavily patterned with dark blotches and spots or even pattern-less. *C. carinata* are typically some shade of beige or brown, with either blotches or a wide continuous but ragged dorsal stripe. Colors may lighten at night. Viper boas exhibit wide brown or black bands on a background of yellow, tan, or reddish-brown. The scales are heavily keeled. Viper boas may prefer higher humidity than the other Pacific boas.

Fiji boa, the largest and most arboreal of the Pacific boas. Coloration and pattern are highly variable.

The stocky, ground-dwelling viper boa, named for its resemblance to the death adder.

The semi-arboreal Pacific ground boa occurs in both a blotched and striped phase. Lizards may be required as food, even as adults.

Pacific boas are now seen fairly regularly at reptile dealers and shows, particularly *C. carinata*. However, most are imported specimens or neonates from imported gravid females. Captive breeding is extremely rare and problematic, possibly related to locality or genetic incompatibility of specimens. Captive maintenance and breeding requirements are similar to other boas, taking into account the degree of arboreal preference of the species being kept. Neonates may be difficult to get started, preferring tiny geckos or other lizards or frogs, or parts thereof, for food. Some specimens may prefer lizards exclusively, even as adults.

The Future of Herpetoculture

A Bright Today, and a Brighter Tomorrow

The future of herpetoculture is very bright, but not without its share of storm clouds on the horizon. As the number of reptile enthusiasts continues to grow, so too does our understanding of these complex animals. Advances in heating, feeding, nutrition, caging, health, medicine, and breeding are sure to continue as we strive to live up to our responsibilities to our pets. Product manufacturers, taking note of the rapidly growing market and the needs of reptiles, have begun creating products that turn these needs into solutions, and take much of the guesswork out of maintaining healthy animals. The proliferation of books and magazines means that the necessary information is right at our fingertips. Whether you're a serious collector or a single-snake pet owner, the tools required to ensure our pets long, healthy lives are all available right now, and will only get better.

Growth of the Hobby

For better or for worse, the rapid growth of herpetoculture has finally brought the hobby out into the open. There is no doubt that seeing or reading news accounts of several thousand enthusiasts attending a local reptile show must make a lot of people wonder if maybe they're missing something. Snakes cannot tell people that they are actually terrific animals, and few people are willing to get close enough to discover the fact on their own. Individuals and herpetological societies have tried chipping away at ignorance for many years. Maybe now, when enough of us say, "Hey, we love these things!," attitudes will start changing on a grand scale. But with all this exposure comes increased scrutiny as well.

When live animals are involved, some scrutiny is not only necessary, but welcome. The level of insensitivity, and even cruelty, of some people in their pursuit of money can be shocking. Regardless of our definition of "animal rights," any decent human being would agree that animals should be provided with their basic needs of food, water, the proper temperature, and reasonable avoidance of stress to the best extent possible. There has probably never been any human endeavor that hasn't been hurt by a few bad apples, and herpetoculture is no exception. Most of our publicity has been and continues to be bad, usually involving accidents or escapes of venomous or giant snakes. In warm climates such as my home state of Florida, the problem has become not escapes, but *releases*, as more and more people impulsively buy large snakes (not to mention iguanas and monitors) that they are not prepared to care for. Every incident provides your neighbors and animal rights groups with ammunition to use in getting reptile-keeping banned. For the sake of all herpetoculturists, take your responsibility as a reptile owner seriously.

To many, preserving a species is as easy as protecting it from killing or collecting in the wild. Yet we are all well aware of the destruction of the world's rain forests and other wild places, and that the plants and animals living there are being lost forever. Through captive breeding, we can ensure the survival of a species even after its habitat is gone, as well as reduce the demand for wild animals even where the habitat is not threatened. But the time to act is now, not when a species is on the brink. If, for instance, an endangered species of boa is found to be difficult to feed or breed in captivity, research on wild populations may provide the answers. If we wait to pull the last 50 boas out just before the last tree falls, it will be too late. In my opinion, countries that bow to pressure to ban all export of wildlife are doing that wildlife a grave disservice, unless they can be absolutely assured of the continued protection of critical habitat as well. Sustainable use can also provide income for indigenous peoples, an added incentive to preserve habitat for long-term benefits over the destruction of slash-and-burn farming.

Few herpetoculturists would disagree that current shipping practices for imported reptiles are in need of improvement. Too many reptiles are being packed together, often without food or water, for too long. Importers and herpetocultural groups are going to have to work with federal and international wildlife agencies to formulate meaningful and reasonable regulations regarding the reptile trade, or face the possibility of an outright ban favored by animal rights groups.

The Circle of Life: Herpetoculture in a Perfect World

In the herpetocultural future I would like to see, countries would vigorously protect and manage entire critical ecosystems, allowing only scientifically determined and sustainable levels of tourism and harvest that do not upset the natural balance. Reptiles would be collected in limited numbers for export by licensed and inspected exporters, and shipped quickly under humane conditions to their destinations. Licensed importers would then inspect shipments upon arrival, and be responsible for proper care during any quarantine period. Stiff fines and revocation of licenses would be actively pursued for repeated violations. Breeders would propagate species, maintaining genetic diversity while reducing the need for importation to a few animals for new bloodlines. Pet shops and reptile dealers would distribute information and care sheets, including a warning regarding maximum size, with each reptile sold. Reptile owners would learn all they could about their pets by reading books and magazines, ensuring them the long, healthy life they deserve. Serious herpetoculturists would join and be active in their local herpetological society, sharing their experiences with others and promoting the benefits and preservation of reptiles through public exhibits and the support of local research, educational, or conservation projects. And finally, we would all remember where our reptiles originally came from, and financially support such worthy organizations as the Nature Conservancy, whose efforts to protect entire critical ecosystems in North, Central, and South America are unequaled. As skilled as we are at propagating species, I'd still like to see Mother Nature continue doing it her own way as well. The circle would be complete.

Useful Literature and Addresses

Books

Today's herpetoculturist can fill an entire shelf with the plethora of available books on the subject. For whatever reptile you are into, and even whatever individual species you are interested in, you will probably find a useful book on the subject. There are also books on specific areas of reptile care, such as feeding, breeding, diseases, and parasites, and medical treatment. All can contribute to your success as a reptile owner. For boa owners who wish to breed their snakes, I highly recommend obtaining a copy of *The Reproductive Husbandry of Pythons and Boas*, by Dr. Richard Ross and Gerald Marzec, published by the Institute for Herpetological Research, 500 Ninos Drive, Santa Barbara, CA 93103.

Pet shops and book stores carry a number of basic books on snakes, but for a more complete selection of titles, both current and out-of-print, contact one of the following book distributors:

Maryland Reptile Farm
  109 W. Cherry Hill Rd.
  Reisterstown, MD 21136
  (410) 526-4184

The Pet Bookshop
  P.O. Box 507
  Oyster Bay, NY 11711
  (516) 922-1169

Zoo Book Sales
  464 Second St.
  Excelsior, MN 55331
  (612) 470-8733

Two recent books published in the Barron's Pet Owner's Manual series about caring for snakes as pets are:

Markel, Ronald G. and Richard Bartlett. *Kingsnakes and Milksnakes,* Barron's Educational Series, Inc., Hauppauge, NY: 1995.

Bartlett, Richard and Patti Bartlett. *Corn Snakes and Other Rat Snakes,* Barron's Educational Series, Inc., Hauppauge, NY: 1996.

Magazines

Full-color reptile magazines offer timely information, keeping pet owners up to date on the latest methods and breakthroughs in husbandry and breeding. Magazines are also a window to the whole spectrum of herpetoculture—the people, animals, products, events, and news. Pick up a copy at your local pet shop or reptile store, and consider getting a subscription. The leading magazines today are:

Reptile and Amphibian Magazine
  RD #3, Box 3709-A
  Pottsville, PA 17901
  (717) 622-6050

Reptiles Magazine
  P.O. Box 58700
  Boulder, CO 80322
  (303) 666-8504

The Vivarium
Published by the American
Federation of Herpetoculturists
P.O. Box 300067
Escondido, CA 92030
(619) 747-4948

Reptile Hobbyist
One TFH Plaza
Neptune City, NJ 07753
(908) 988-8400

Reptilian Magazine
22 Firs Close
Hazlemere, High Wycombe
Bucks HP15 7TF, England

Herpetological Societies

Joining your local herpetological society is a great way to meet people who share your interests. Most societies are comprised of a mix of enthusiasts, pet owners, breeders and researchers, both young and old. Monthly meetings may feature interesting discussions or guest speakers, and offer an excellent opportunity for you to get answers to your questions. Many societies also publish a newsletter for paid members. To find out if there is a herp society in your area, make inquiries at pet shops that offer reptiles for sale, or check one of the directories described later.

Professional and Scientific Journals

The following professional herpetological societies publish journals of a more technical nature, dealing with topics of natural history, behavior, morphology, taxonomy, conservation and other scientific research.

Society for the Study of Amphibians
and Reptiles (SSAR)
Publishes *Journal of Herpetology*
and *Herpetological Review*
P.O. Box 626
Hays, KS 67601

American Society of Ichthyologists and
Herpetologists (ASIH)
Publishes *Copeia*
Department of Zoology
Southern Illinois University
Carbondale, IL 62901

The Herpetologists League
Publishes *Herpetologica*
Department of Biological Sciences
Box 70726
East Tennessee State University
Johnson City, TN 37614

Directories

Herpetological directories provide an organized listing of who's who and what's what in herpetoculture. If you know what you want, a good directory will tell you where you can find it—breeders, publications, herp societies, wholesalers, reptile stores, shows, product manufacturers, rodent suppliers, cage builders, and even zoos and reptile exhibits—and are typically updated and reprinted every two years. Herpetological directories are available from the following sources:

Reptile and Amphibian Magazine
RD #3, Box 3709-A
Pottsville, PA 17901
(717) 622-6050

Great Valley Serpentarium
2379 Maggio Circle, Unit C
Lodi, CA 95240
(209) 369-7737

Shows and Symposiums

Reptile shows are an excellent way for pet owners to meet and talk with breeders and product manufacturers face-to-face. For the sheer variety of animals and expertise available, there is nothing like them. Some of the larger shows attract hundreds of exhibitors from all over the country and thousands of herpetoculturists. Symposiums are a series of educational lectures presented by notable breeders and researchers, often non-commercial but occasionally held in conjunction with a reptile show or fund-raising auction. A schedule of upcoming herpetocultural events can be found in most reptile magazines.

Cruising the Information Superhighway

Herpetoculture has not been left out of the computer revolution. First came bulletin board systems (BBS's) dedicated to herpetoculturists, where by dialing up by modem one could post questions and upload or download files. Online services such as America Online and Prodigy continued the trend with their own reptile topics in their bulletin boards. The introduction of chat rooms eliminated the delay between posting questions and receiving answers, allowing instantaneous discussion with others. Today, a number of breeders, publications, manufacturers, and distributors are creating their own home pages on the World Wide Web, or Internet. Try your web browser on some herp terms and see what comes up.

Glossary

Ambient Pertaining to external surrounding conditions, such as temperature or light.

Arboreal Tree-dwelling.

Basking Resting in an area of heat or light.

Boidae Taxonomic family of snakes that includes the boas and pythons.

Boids Snakes of the family *Boidae*; boas and pythons.

Breeding trials Introducing males and females together for the purpose of breeding.

Brumation A state of inactivity and reduced metabolism, but to a lesser degree than hibernation.

CITES Convention on International Trade in Endangered Species.

Cloaca Chamber into which the digestive, urinary, and reproductive canals open; it then opens to the exterior through the anal vent at the base of the tail.

Colubrids Snakes of the family *Colubridae*, including most common nonvenomous, non-boid species.

Combat Competition between males for dominance and breeding rights, usually consisting of intertwining and forcing an opponent to the ground.

Diurnal Pertaining to daytime; pertaining to animals active by day.

Dorsal Pertaining to the back; along the spine.

Ecdysis Periodic shedding of the epidermis.

Ectothermic Cold-blooded; dependent on external sources for body heat.

Eyecap Clear, curved scale that protects a snake's eyes.

Fossorial Burrowing underground.

Founders Animals representing new genetic bloodlines.

Full-spectrum light Light closely imitating sunlight, including ultraviolet wavelengths important to many reptiles.

Fuzzies Young rodents just beginning to grow hair.

Gestation Period in which eggs or neonates develop within the female's body.

Gradient Range or gradual change, such as a temperature gradient from warm to cool.

Gravid Term used to describe a reptile carrying fertilized eggs or young.

Hemipenis One of two paired copulatory organs of male snakes and lizards; pl. hemipenes.

Herpetoculture Hobby or business of keeping reptiles and/or amphibians.

Herpetology Scientific study of reptiles and amphibians.

Heterozygous Lacking pure genes for a given trait; carrying a recessive gene.

Homozygous Carrying pure genes for a given trait.

Insular Pertaining to islands.

Jacobson's organ Sensory organ located in the palate where airborne particles are transferred from the tongue for identification.

Lateral Pertaining to the sides.

Mites Tiny blood-sucking external parasites.

Morph Inheritable color or pattern variation; phase.

Neonates Newborn or hatchling.

Nocturnal Pertaining to nighttime; pertaining to animals active at night.

Opaque Cloudy; preparing to shed.

Ovoviviparous Reproduction by membraned eggs in which embryos develop within the female's body, receiving nourishment from the egg yolk, not from a placental connection.

Parasite loading Build-up of internal or external parasites resulting from confinement.

Parturition Act of giving birth or laying eggs.

Phase Inheritable color or pattern variation; morph.

Photoperiod Period of light and dark within a day.

Pinkies Hairless newborn rodents; in rats also called pups.

Probing Technique used to determine the gender of snakes, involving insertion of a blunt probe into the base of the tail; males probe deeper than females.

Quarantine Period of isolation and observation for new animals to prevent introduction of disease or parasites into a healthy, established collection.

Shedding Periodic sloughing of the epidermis.

Spurs Small claws, remnants of hind limbs, present on either side of the cloaca in many boas and pythons; when present, they are often larger in males.

Substrate Any material used to line the bottom of cages.

Taxonomy Systematics; branch of biology dealing with scientific classification of living organisms and their evolutionary relationships.

Temperate Having a well-defined seasonal variation in temperature.

Terrestrial Ground-dwelling.

Vent Anal or cloacal opening in reptiles.

Ventral Pertaining to the belly, or underside; the long scales on the underside of a snake, used in locomotion.

Bibliography

de Vosjoli, Philippe, *The General Care and Maintenance of Red-Tailed Boas*, Advanced Vivarium Systems, 1990.

Klingenburg, Roger J., *Understanding Reptile Parasites*, Advanced Vivarium Systems, 1993.

Kluge, Arnold, *Boine snake phylogeny and research cycles*, University of Michigan, 1991.

Kluge, Arnold, *Calabaria and the phylogeny of erycine snakes*, Zoological Journal of the Linnean Society, 1993.

Mattison, Chris, *Encyclopedia of Snakes*, Facts on File, 1995.

Mehrtens, John, *Living Snakes of the World in Color*, Sterling Publishing Company, 1987

McDowell, Sam, *Snakes, Ecology and Evolutionary Biology*, Macmillan Publishing Company, 1987.

Ross, Richard A., *The Bacterial Diseases of Reptiles*, Institute for Herpetological Research, 1984.

Ross, Richard A. and Gerald Marzec, *The Reproductive Husbandry of Pythons and Boas*, Institute for Herpetological Research, 1990.

Spiteri, David G., *Current Taxonomy and Captive Breeding of the Rosy Boa*, The Vivarium, American Federation of Herpetoculturists, Vol. 5 No. 3, 1993.

Index